Copyright © 2o21 by Marcos Manor -All rights reserved.

No part of this publication may be reproduced, distributed, or transmitted in any form or by any means, including photocopying, recording, or other electronic or mechanical methods, without the prior written permission of the publisher, except in the case of brief quotations embodied in reviews and certain other non-commercial uses permitted by copyright law.

This Book is provided with the sole purpose of providing relevant information on a specific topic for which every reasonable effort has been made to ensure that it is both accurate and reasonable. Nevertheless, by purchasing this Book you consent to the fact that the author, as well as the publisher, are in no way experts on the topics contained herein, regardless of any claims as such that may be made within. It is recommended that you always consult a professional prior to undertaking any of the advice or techniques discussed within.This is a legally binding declaration that is considered both valid and fair by both the Committee of Publishers Association and the American Bar Association and should be considered as legally binding within the United States.

CONTENTS

INTRODUCTION 6
    Ninja Foodi: How It Simplifies Your Life 6
    Benefits Of Family Meals 6
    What Exactly Does The Ninja Foodi Do? 8

APPETIZERS & SNACKS 10
    Asian Spiced Chicken Wings 10
    Bacon Cheeseburger Dip 11
    BBQ Oysters with Bacon 12
    Cheesy Artichoke & Crab Dip 13
    Cinnamon Apple Chips 14
    Easy Crab Wontons 15
    Hot Pepper Jelly Cheese Dip with Bacon 16
    Jalapeno & Cheese Wontons 17
    Lemon Pepper Wings 18
    Rum Spiced Nuts 19
    Salsa Verde Slow Cooker Dip 20
    Southwest Chicken Egg Rolls 21
    Spicy Cauliflower Bites 22

BREAKFAST 23
    Almond French Toast Bites 23
    Baked Biscuits & Gravy 24
    Blueberry Bagels 25
    Breakfast Stuffed Baked Potatoes 26
    Caramel Pumpkin Oatmeal 27
    Cheesy Ham & Egg Casserole 28
    Cherry Fritters 29
    Double Meat Breakfast Casserole 30
    Easy Glazed Doughnuts 31
    Eggs Benedict Bread Pudding 32
    French Toast & Cream Cheese Casserole 34

 Maple Sausage Bread Pudding 35

 Sausage and Spinach Breakfast Casserole 36

 Strawberries & Cream Quinoa 37

 Walnut Date Oatmeal 38

MAIN DISHES 39

 Baked Calamari & Shrimp Pasta 39

 Beer Braised Brisket 41

 Cheesy Shepherd's Pie 42

 Chicken Poblano 44

 Chicken Potato & Broccoli Casserole 45

 Chipotle Chicken Bowls 46

 Crab Frittata 47

 Creamy Braised Oxtails 48

 Duck Confit 49

 Easy Baked Beef & Pasta 50

 Korean Chicken 51

 Lamb Marsala 52

 Pork Loin with Onion Beer Sauce 53

 Sausage Onions & Peppers 54

 Seafood Casserole 55

 Speedy Paella 56

 Southwest Short Ribs 57

 Sweet & Spicy Balsamic Beef 58

 Thai Sweet Pork 59

 Veal Marengo 60

SIDE DISHES 61

 Baked Beans 61

 Braised Artichokes 62

 Carrot Pudding 63

 Cheesy Green Chili Rice 64

 Creamy Cheesy Polenta 65

Holiday Brussels Sprouts with Nuts & Cranberries 66
Lemon Orzo with Asparagus 67
Pumpkin & Bacon Risotto 68
Roasted Corn 69
Scalloped Pineapple 70
Soy-Glazed Mushrooms 71
Spicy Red Potatoes 72
Squash with Cherries 73
Teriyaki Green Beans & Mushrooms 74
Zucchini Pasta with Walnuts & Basil 75

SOUPS & STEWS **76**

Autumn Stew 76
Cheesy Onion Soup 77
Creamy Chicken & Mushroom Soup 78
Duck Ale Chili 79
Greens & Beans Soup 80
Irish Lamb Stew 81
Jamaican Chicken Stew 82
Lamb Provencal 83
Mushroom & Wild Rice Soup 84
Poblano Beef Stew 85
Sausage & Spinach Stew 86
Seafood Stew 87
Shrimp & Mango Curry 88
Sunchoke & Asparagus Soup 89
Sweet Potato & Black Bean Stew 90
Tipsy Potato Chowder 91
Tuscan-Style Veggie Soup 92
Venison Stew 93
Verde Pork Stew 94
White Chicken Chili 95

DESSERTS 96

- Banana Bundt Cake 96
- Bananas Foster 97
- Blackberry Brioche Bread Pudding 98
- Blueberry & Peach Streusel Pie 99
- Caramel Apple Chimichangas 100
- Cherry Cobbler 101
- Chocolate Pecan Pie 102
- Coconut Cream Cake 103
- Hot Fudge Cake 104
- Individual S'Mores Pies 105
- Lemon Sponge Pie 106
- Meyer Lemon Hand Pies 107
- Noodle Kugel 109
- Pineapple Pecan Bread Pudding 110
- Reece's Cookie Bars 111
- Super Simple Chocolate Brownies 112
- Turtle Fudge Pudding 113

INTRODUCTION

Ninja Foodi: How It Simplifies Your Life

So, you got one of those newfangled Ninja Foodi's, congratulations! If you bought it for yourself, go ahead and give yourself a big pat on the back. If you got it as a gift, make sure you say a big thank-you to the wonderful person who bought it for you. Now, you are probably wondering just what to do with this fancy cooker. Well, that is where this book comes in. I am sure you have seen those other combination cookers that have changed the culinary world. Chances are a friend or family member has one and has told you all about it. Well, this new cook from Ninja is going make those friends and family members extremely jealous. The Ninja Foodi does everything the previous brands do, plus so much more. It is going to revolutionize the way you look at cooking. Many people view cooking for their families as a necessary chore, not as something that should bring them pride and joy. One reason for that is we are way too busy to take pleasure in the beauty of preparing a well cooked meal.

Plus, we are so busy that by the end of the day, who feels like cooking? Just stopping by that fast food restaurant that is on the way home, is so much easier. But it isn't better for you or your family. It is time we stopped settling for easy and started creating more healthy meals shared with our families. America has the highest rates of diabetes, obesity and heart disease on the planet. We trade in healthy, home cooked meals for the convenience of fast food full of grease, fat and other things we probably don't want to know about. But it is extremely important that we stop this rat race and spend time around the dinner table together again.

A number of studies have been done that prove there are many benefits to gathering around the table to eat together as a family.

Benefits Of Family Meals

1. Family dinners pave the way for better family relationships. Dinner together is the perfect opportunity for everyone to share their days and catch up with other family members. For young children, regular family meals provide them with both security and feeling safe. And, while they may not admit it, teenagers enjoy the chance to talk about their lives in a safe setting.

2. Family meals teach better food choices. Kids that eat meals with their families eat more fruits and vegetables and consume less soda and fried foods. Eating together teaches your children how to make healthy food choices that can help them lead a healthy lifestyle as they grow.

3. Eating together leads to better grades. A few studies have been done that show that family meals help school age children to do better in school. One report by CASA showed that teens who ate at least 5 family meals a week brought in A's and B's, whereas those with less family time also had lower grades.

4. Family meals provide a way to expose your kids to new foods. You can encourage them to try new things and by doing so expand their tastes.

5. Family meals leads to more happiness. Teens who eat with their families tend to be happier, well-adjusted, show better communication skills and overall have a better mental health than those who do not. Mothers who eat with their children tend be less stressed or overwhelmed and also happier.

6. Home cooked meals provide portion control. Obesity is a huge problem in our youth today. Restaurant portions are way larger than what a body needs to consume. By cooking at home you can make sure they eat only what they need to be healthy.

7. Eating at home saves you money. On average it costs about $8 per person for fast food. While cooking a meal at home averages out to $4.50 a meal at home.

So the next big questions is, how do we cook more healthy meals at home with our limited amount of time? Answer, the Ninja Foodi!

What Exactly Does The Ninja Foodi Do?

Your combination cooker reduces the amount of time you spend in the kitchen cooking delicious, healthy meals, so you can spend more quality time with the ones you love. The pressure cooking functions cuts most cooking times by one third, to one half of traditional cooking methods. It also forces the juices into the food, so for instance, tougher cuts of meat turn out melt-in-your mouth tender. It slow cooks, again this saves you time since you can just throw the ingredients in the cooker, push a couple of buttons and walk away. Dinner is done when you get home from work, or breakfast is ready when you wake up in the morning. The Ninja Foodi has a steamer for cooking rice, fancy steamed puddings or plump, delicious dumplings. You can quickly steam your favorite vegetables without losing any of their nutrients, like you do when you boil them.

It has a saute function with multiple heat settings. So you can saute, fry and cook easy one pot meals at the push of a button. But, wait, there's more!

Unlike the other popular one pot cookers, the Foodi is even more complete. It has a built in air fryer! So now you can create delicious, crispy fried food without adding any fat, calories or cholesterol to your favorite recipes. Make the perfect fish and chips, crunchy French fries, onion rings and even fluffy homemade doughnuts. With the addition of the Tender Crisp lid, in just a few seconds you can turn your cooker into a mini over. It has all the same temperatures as your standard oven does, but it uses half the electricity. So, now it saves you money too! With the tender crisp lid you can bake casseroles and desserts. It broils, and it even dehydrates, so you can make your own jerky or dried fruits at home. The inner cooking pot is made from durable, non-stick ceramic so clean up is a breeze.

It comes with a reversible rack, so you can cook multiple types of food all at one time. Not only do you cut down on cooking time, but now you cut down on the cleanup time as well. It's a win-win. In this book you will find 100 fun, tasty recipes that will turn you into a Foodi expert in no time. In the Appetizers & Snacks chapter there are recipes for treats like Bacon Cheeseburger Dip and Easy Crab Wontons. Breakfast covers both sweet and savory with recipes for Baked Biscuits & Gravy Casserole to Blueberry Bagels. In the main course chapter you can find easy peasy meals to some of your restaurant favorites, like Duck Confit and Poblano Chicken.

The side dishes chapter covers all kinds of recipes that include vegetables, pasta and rice including Carrot Pudding and Teriyaki Green Beans. In the soups and stews sections are light, healthy soups, like the Greens & Beans Soup, to hearty, comforting stews, like my favorite Venison Stew. And finally, desserts, here you will find everything from cakes, to pies to brownies, including recipes for Banana Bundt Cake and Chocolate Pecan Pie. So, don't be afraid of this new cooking contraption. Roll up your sleeves and start creating dishes that your friends and family will be impressed by. Most of these recipes are kid friendly and will help them to be able to try some new foods in ways they will actually like. No matter what you are making in your new Ninja Foodi, be sure to have fun while you are doing it. Goodness knows we can all use a lot more of that our busy lives.

APPETIZERS & SNACKS

Asian Spiced Chicken Wings

These sticky, spicy wings make a great light lunch, or make more than the recipe calls for and serve them for game day.

Yields: 2 servings

Prep Time: 5 mins

Cook Time: 30 mins

Ingredients:

- 8 chicken wings
- 2 tablespoons soy sauce
- 2 tablespoons Chinese spice
- Salt & pepper

Preparation instructions:

1. Add the soy sauce, spice, salt and pepper to a large mixing bowl and stir to combine.
2. Add the wings and toss to coat well.
3. Place the rack in the bottom of the cooker. Place the chicken on it and pour any remaining sauce over it.
4. Add the Tender Crisp lid and set the temperature to 350 degrees.
5. Cook for 15 minutes, then turn the chicken over and cook another 15 minutes. Serve with your favorite dipping sauce.

Bacon Cheeseburger Dip

This warm, cheesy dip has all the flavor of the popular bacon cheeseburger. Make up a batch for parties, game day or just a day spent bingeing your favorite TV shows.

Yields: 8 servings

Prep Time: 5 mins

Cook Time: 30 mins

Ingredients:

- 1 pound ground beef
- 1 package cream cheese, soft
- 2 cups cheddar cheese, grated
- 10 ounce can of Rotel tomatoes with green chilies
- 1 cup sour cream
- 2/3 cup bacon, cooked crisp and crumbled

Preparation instructions:

1. Set the cooker to the sauté function on med-high. Add ground beef and cook through, breaking it up while cooking. Drain the fat.
2. Combine remaining ingredients in a large bowl and mix till well combined. Stir in ground beef.
3. Pour into a baking dish that will fit inside the cooking pot. Add the Tender Crisp lid and lock into place.
4. Set the temperature to 350 degrees. Bake for 20 – 25 minutes or hot and bubbly.
5. Serve with your favorite chips or crackers for dipping.

BBQ Oysters with Bacon

This tasty take on oysters will have even the non-fans asking for more. The addition of bacon and horseradish compliment the fresh ocean taste of the oysters.

Yields: 12 oysters

Prep Time: 20 mins

Cook Time: 10 mins

Ingredients:

- 1 dozen fresh oysters, shucked and left on the half shell
- Rock salt
- 1 pound thick cut bacon, sliced into thin strips
- 1/3 cup ketchup
- ¼ cup Worcestershire sauce
- Juice of ½ lemon
- 1 teaspoon horseradish
- Dash of your favorite hot sauce
- Lime wedges for garnish

Preparation instructions:

1. Line a shallow baking dish that will fit inside the cooker with rock salt. Place the oysters snugly into the salt, you will have to cook them in batches.
2. In a large bowl, combine remaining ingredients and mix well.
3. Add a dash of Worcestershire to each oyster then top with bacon mixture.
4. Use the Tender Crisp lid and lock into place. Set the temperature to broil and cook 10 minutes, or till bacon is crisp.
5. Serve with lime wedges.

Cheesy Artichoke & Crab Dip

Serve this hot and tasty dip at your next party or get together and you are sure to impress your friends and family. It combines the delicious flavors of crab dip with cheesy artichoke dip for something divine.

Yields: 4 cups

Prep Time: 15 minutes

Cook Time: 30 minutes

Ingredients:

- 1 pound lump crab meat
- 14 ounce can artichoke hearts, drained
- ¾ cups cheddar cheese, grated
- 1/3 cup Parmesan cheese
- 6 tablespoons sour cream
- 6 tablespoons mayonnaise
- 2 tablespoons chives, chopped
- 1-2 teaspoons hot sauce
- 1 teaspoon lemon juice

Preparation instructions:

1. Chop the artichokes and crab and place them in a mixing bowl. Add the remaining ingredients and mix till combined. Transfer to a baking dish that will fit inside the cooking pot.
2. Add the Tender Crisp lid and lock into place. Set the temperature for 400 degrees and bake 30 minutes or till cheese is melted and top is golden brown.
3. Serve with your favorite chips, crackers or toasted bread

Cinnamon Apple Chips

These tasty chips are a healthier alternative to traditional potato chips. Make them to have handy for after school snacks or to add as a treat to their lunch boxes.

Yields: 2 servings

Prep Time: 5 minutes

Cook Time: 10 minutes

Ingredients:

- 1 medium apple, sliced thin
- ¼ teaspoon cinnamon
- ¼ teaspoon nutmeg

Preparation instructions:

1. Place all ingredients into a mixing bowl and toss to coat the apple slice.
2. Place the apples in the fryer basket, in one layer and add to the cooker.
3. Lock the Tender Crisp lid in place and set the temperature to 375 degrees.
4. Cook for 8 minutes, turning over halfway through
5. Serve immediately or store in an airtight container.

Easy Crab Wontons

Now you can make your favorite take-out appetizers at home. These tasty crab and cheese wontons are easy to make and are ideal to serve with a Chinese inspired meal or as a snack.

Yields: 16 pieces

Prep Time: 10 minutes

Cook Time: 10 minutes

Ingredients:

- 16 wonton wrappers
- ¾ cup lump crab meat
- 2 green onions, chopped
- 3 tablespoons cream cheese, soft
- Black pepper
- Old Bay seasoning

Preparation instructions:

1. Combine all ingredients in a mixing bowl and mix well
2. Lay out wrappers on a work surface. Moisten with a dab of water and spoon about 1 ½ teaspoons filling on each.
3. Pull two opposite corners up over filling and pinch together. Repeat with other corners. Spray the wontons lightly with cooking spray.
4. Spray the cooking pot with and add the wontons, you will have to cook them in batches.
5. Lock the Tender Crisp lid in place and set temperature to 350 degrees. Cook 8 minutes or till they are golden brown and crisp.
6. Serve with your favorite dipping sauce or enjoy them on their own.

Hot Pepper Jelly Cheese Dip with Bacon

This dip is both sweet and salty with just a touch of heat. It is ideal for holiday parties with its festive color and taste.

Yields: 2 cups

Prep Time: 10 minutes

Cook Time: 35 minutes

Ingredients:

- 1 10.5 ounce jar hot pepper Jelly
- 1 package cream cheese, soft
- 1 cup sharp cheddar cheese, grated
- 4 slices bacon, cooked crisp and crumbled
- 1 clove garlic, chopped fine
- 1/2 teaspoon salt

Preparation instructions:

1. Beat cream cheese in a large bowl till creamy. Add cheddar, garlic, and salt and mix well. Stir in ½ the jelly till well combined.
2. Lightly grease a baking dish that will fit inside the cooker. Pour the mixture in the dish.
3. Place the rack in the bottom of the cooker and place the dip on top. Lock on the Tender Crisp lid and set the temperature to 350 degrees.
4. Bake 35 – 40 minutes or till hot and bubbly. Carefully remove the dip from the cooker
5. Slightly melt the remaining jelly in the microwave and spread over the top of the dip and top with the bacon. Serve warm with crackers or pita chips.

Jalapeno & Cheese Wontons

All the flavor of a jalapeno popper wrapped up into a crispy wonton. These make ideal appetizers for a party, get together or as a special treat for movie night.

Yields: 16 – 20 pieces

Prep Time: 10 minutes

Cook Time: 15 minutes

Ingredients:

- 1 package wonton wrappers
- 1 package cream cheese, soft
- 3 jalapenos, remove ribs and seeds and chop fine
- ½ cup cheddar cheese, grated
- Coarse salt

Preparation instructions:

1. In a bowl, combine cream cheese, jalapenos, and cheddar cheese.
2. Lay out wrappers on a work surface. Moisten with a dab of water and spoon about 1 ½ teaspoons filling on each.
3. Pull two opposite corners up over filling and pinch together. Repeat with other corners. Spray the wontons lightly with cooking spray.
4. Spray the cooking pot with and add the wontons, you will have to cook them in batches.
5. Lock the Tender Crisp lid in place and set temperature to 350 degrees. Cook 8 minutes or till they are golden brown and crisp.
6. Sprinkle with salt and serve warm

Lemon Pepper Wings

These have all the flavor of your favorite sports bar. Crispy wings popping with the fresh taste of lemon and a kick of heat from the pepper.

Yields: 4 servings

Prep Time: 10 minutes

Cook Time: 20 minutes

Ingredients:

- 2 ½ pounds chicken wing pieces
- 1 cup flour
- 1/3 cup butter
- 1 teaspoon lemon pepper
- ½ teaspoon salt
- ½ teaspoon black pepper

Preparation instructions:

1. Mix flour with salt in pepper in a large bowl. Add wing pieces, in small batches to flour and toss to coat each piece well.

2. Spray the fryer basket lightly with cooking spray. Add wings, in batches, to basket and place in the cooker. Lock the Tender Crisp lid in place and set temperature to 360 degrees.

3. Cook for 10 minutes, then turn the wings over and cook an additional 10 minutes or till they are golden brown.

4. Place the butter in a medium mixing bowl and melt in the microwave. Stir in the lemon pepper seasoning and then add cooked wings and toss to coat.

5. Serve with your favorite dipping sauce.

Rum Spiced Nuts

Sweet, spiced nuts are traditionally made around the holidays. But once you taste these you will want to keep them on hand for snacking all year round. These savory nuts get their special flavor from the dark rum.

Yields: 3 cups

Prep Time: 5 minutes

Cook Time: 10 minutes

Ingredients:

- 3 cups mixed nuts
- 2 tablespoons butter
- 2 tablespoons dark rum
- 2 tablespoons sugar
- 1 tablespoon salt
- 2 teaspoons curry powder
- 1 teaspoon ancho chile powder
- 1 teaspoon cinnamon
- 1 teaspoon cumin

Preparation instructions:

1. Set the cooker to sauté on medium heat. Add nuts and cook to lightly toast them, about 3-5 minutes, stirring frequently.
2. Add the butter and rum to the nuts and cook, stirring frequently, till most of the liquid evaporates and the nuts are glassy.
3. In a large bowl, add remaining ingredients and stir to combine. Add the glazed nuts and toss well to coat.
4. Dump the nuts onto a large baking sheet to cool. Serve immediately or store in an airtight container.

Salsa Verde Slow Cooker Dip

This ooey, gooey salsa dip is ideal for dunking more than just tortilla chips. The dip is made from four kinds of cheese and is a tasty dip for chicken tenders, pretzels or lightly toasted pieces of bread, like a baguette.

Yields: 8 – 10 servings

Prep Time: 10 minutes

Cook Time: 2 hours

Ingredients:

- ½ cup salsa verde
- ½ cup green chilies, diced
- ½ package cream cheese, soft
- ½ cup white American cheese, cubed
- ½ cup white cheddar cheese, cubed
- ½ cup pepper Jack cheese, cubed
- ¼ cup milk

Preparation instructions:

1. Combine all ingredients in mixing bowl and mix till combined.
2. Pour into a small baking dish that will fit inside the cooker.
3. Lock the lid in place and select slow cooker function on high. Set the timer for 2 hours, but stir the dip every 30 minutes. Cook till all the cheese is completely melted.

Southwest Chicken Egg Rolls

These delicious egg rolls are filled with a Mexican filling with a just the right amount of heat. The filling combines chicken cheese and peppers for a tasty bite that is sure to please your guests at your next party.

Yields: 6 pieces

Prep Time: 15 minutes

Cook Time: 20 minutes

Ingredients:

- 6 egg roll wrappers
- 1 cup Mexican blend cheese, grated
- ½ cup chicken, cooked and shredded
- ½ cup red onion, chopped fine
- ½ cup bell pepper, chopped fine
- ½ cup fire roasted tomatoes, drained
- ½ avocado, chopped fine
- 1 teaspoon chili powder
- 1 teaspoon olive oil
- Water

Preparation instructions:

1. Set cooker to saute setting on med-high heat. Add olive oil and red onion. Cook, stirring frequently till onion becomes translucent.
2. Add bell peppers and cook 2-3 minutes. Add tomatoes and cook an additional 2-3 minutes, stirring frequently.
3. Transfer vegetables to a bowl and mix in the remaining ingredients till blended.
4. Place wrappers on a work surface. Place about 2 tablespoons of filling near one corner. Fold the corner closest to the filling over it. Fold both side corners toward the center and roll it up. Seal with water. Lightly spray the rolls with cooking spray on both sides.
5. Wipe out the cooker. Lightly spray the rack with cooking spray and place it into the pot. Place egg rolls on the rack and lock the Tender Crisp lid in place.
6. Set the temperature for 375 degrees and cook egg rolls for 8 minutes. Flip them over and cook another 8 minutes or till golden brown.

Spicy Cauliflower Bites

All the yummy flavor of Buffalo wings without all the fat and calories. These are a healthy version of wings and they are so good even the kids will ask for more.

Yields: 4 servings

Prep Time: 5 mins

Cook Time: 10 mins

Ingredients:

- 1 cup panko bread crumbs
- 1 cup ranch dressing
- ½ head of cauliflower, separated into florets
- ½ cup hot sauce
- 1 egg
- ½ teaspoon salt
- ½ teaspoon garlic powder
- Black pepper

Preparation instructions:

1. Place the egg in a medium bowl and mix in the salt, pepper and garlic. Place the panko crumbs into a small bowl.
2. Dip the florets first in the egg then into the panko crumbs.
3. Place the basket into the cooker and add breaded cauliflower. Lock the Tender Crisp lid in place and set the temperature to 400 degrees.
4. Cook the cauliflower for 8 – 10 minutes, shaking half way through, or till crisp and golden brown.
5. Mix the ranch dressing with the hot sauce and serve it for dipping.

BREAKFAST

Almond French Toast Bites

Crispy little bites covered with cinnamon sugar and with a subtle flavor of almond. These are ideal for a weekend breakfast the kids will love.

Yields: 3 serving

Prep Time: 5 minutes

Cook Time: 15 minutes

Ingredients:

- 8 pieces of bread
- 6 eggs
- 1/3 cup sugar
- 2 tablespoons almond milk
- 2 tablespoons cinnamon

Preparation instructions:

1. Whisk the eggs and almond milk together in a small bowl.
2. In a separate small bowl mix the sugar and cinnamon together.
3. Tear the bread in half and roll the halves into balls, pressing them firmly together.
4. Soak the balls in the egg till it starts to soak into the bread, then roll them in the cinnamon sugar.
5. Place the balls, 8 at a time, in the basket for the air fryer. Lock the Tender Crisp lid in place and set the temperature to 360 degrees. Cook the bites 15 minutes, or till they are crisp.
6. Serve them with maple syrup for dipping or eat them as they are.

Baked Biscuits & Gravy

A quick and easy way to make biscuits and gravy for a delicious weekend breakfast or brunch. This breakfast casserole has all of the components of a full breakfast in each tasty bite.

Yields: 4 servings

Prep Time: 10 minutes

Cook Time: 1 hour

Ingredients:

- 1 tube refrigerated biscuits
- 1 pound sausage, cooked and drained
- 4 eggs
- 1 cup cheddar cheese, grated
- 1/3 cup milk
- ½ teaspoon pepper
- ½ teaspoon salt

For the gravy

- 2 cups milk
- 4 tablespoons butter
- 4 tablespoons flour
- ½ teaspoon salt
- ½ teaspoon pepper

Preparation instructions:

1. Cut each biscuit into 8 pieces. Set aside.
2. Mix the eggs, milk, salt and pepper in a bowl till combined.
3. Set the cooker to sauté on medium heat. Add butter and melt. Stir in flour, salt and pepper and while stirring, slowly pour in the milk.
4. Increase the heat to med-high and simmer gravy till it thickens. Transfer to a small bowl.
5. Wipe out the inside of the cooker and spray it lightly with cooking spray.
6. Add biscuit pieces to the cooker, then add sausage, cheese, egg mix and top with gravy.
7. Lock the Tender Crisp lid in place and set the temperature to 350 degrees. Bake for 35 – 45 minutes or eggs are cooked through.

Blueberry Bagels

Delicious, airy bagels just like the ones you get at your favorite bakery. Once you make these at home you will never buy the store bought ones again. You can substitute the blueberries for other fruit, or leave it out and add in some cinnamon!

Yields: 4 bagels

Prep time: 10 mins

Cook time: 25 mins

Ingredients:

- 1 cup flour
- 1 cup yogurt
- ¼ cup dried blueberries
- 2 tablespoons sugar
- 1 egg white
- 2 teaspoons baking powder
- 2 teaspoons water
- ¼ teaspoon sea salt

Preparation instructions:

1. Combine dry ingredients, except berries, in a small bowl.
2. In a medium bowl, stir together the yogurt and berries. Fold in the dry ingredients till combined.
3. Knead the dough, on a lightly floured surface, several times till it is no longer sticky. Cut it into 4 pieces and roll each piece into an 8-inch long rope.
4. In a separate small bowl, stir together the egg white and water.
5. Form a loop with each dough piece and pinch the ends together.
6. Brush with the egg white mixture and add them to the fryer basket, 2 at a time.
7. Lock the Tender Crisp lid in place and set the temperature to 330 degrees. Bake 12 minutes, then repeat with remaining bagels.
8. Serve warm or let cool and store tightly wrapped for later.

Breakfast Stuffed Baked Potatoes

Here is a new twist on breakfast. Baked potatoes stuffed with bacon, eggs and cheese then topped with avocado. Since the potatoes bake overnight they are quick and easy to make in the morning.

Yields: 4 servings

Prep Time: 5 minutes

Cook Time: 8 hours 10 minutes

Ingredients:

- 4 potatoes, scrubbed and pricked all over
- 4 strips bacon, cooked and crumbled
- 4 eggs
- ½ cup cheddar cheese, grated
- 1 avocado, sliced
- ¼ cup chives, chopped
- 1 teaspoon olive oil
- Salt & pepper

Preparation instructions:

1. Rub the potatoes with oil and sprinkle with salt and pepper. Wrap in foil and place them in the cooking pot. Lock the lid in place and select slow cooking function on low heat. Cook potatoes overnight.
2. In the morning, carefully remove the potatoes and set the cooker to saute on med-high heat. Cook bacon till crisp, drain on paper towel and crumble when cool enough to do so.
3. Fry the eggs how you like them.
4. To assemble, cut the potatoes open, sprinkle cheese over them. Top with bacon, an egg, a slice of avocado and the chives. Salt and pepper to taste and enjoy.

Caramel Pumpkin Oatmeal

This creamy, delicious oatmeal is perfect for Fall when pumpkin everything is in season. You can even make it gluten free if needed by using gluten free oats, or dairy free by substituting almond or coconut milk for the regular dairy.

Yields: 10 servings

Prep Time: 5 minutes

Cook Time: 2 hours

Ingredients:

- 5 -7 cups milk
- 2 cups rolled oats
- ½ cup pumpkin
- ½ cup date paste
- 2 teaspoon cinnamon
- ½ teaspoon ginger
- ¼ teaspoon nutmeg

Preparation instructions:

1. Add all ingredients to the cooking pot. Secure the lid and select slow cooker function on high heat. Set timer for 2 hours.
2. Stir before serving. Store any left overs in an airtight container in the refrigerator.

Cheesy Ham & Egg Casserole

This hearty breakfast casserole is a great way to start the day. One of the best things about it is you can start it before you go to bed and wake up to a delicious breakfast. A great recipe for those busy mornings.

Yields: 8 servings

Prep Time: 5 minutes

Cook Time: 4 -8 hours

Ingredients:

- 1 bag O'Brien potatoes, frozen
- 1 dozen eggs
- ½ pound ham, diced
- 1 cup cheddar cheese, grated
- ½ cup milk
- Salt & pepper

Preparation instructions:

1. Lightly spray the inside of the cooking pot with cooking spray.
2. Place the potatoes in the pot. Then top with ham and the cheese.
3. Beat the eggs in a large bowl. Stir in milk, salt and pepper and pour over the other ingredients.
4. Secure the lid and select slow cooker function. The casserole will be done in 4 hours on high heat or 8 hours on low.

Cherry Fritters

Cherry fritters make for a special breakfast treat. By cooking them in the air fryer, you can eliminate a lot of the fat and calories, which makes them even better. These are best on the day you make them or freeze them for later.

Yields: 12 fritters
Prep Time: 30 minutes
Cook Time: 30 minutes
Ingredients:

- 2 ¾ cups flour
- 1 ¼ cups sweet cherries, pitted and chopped
- 1 cup milk
- 1 egg
- 3 tablespoons sugar
- 2 tablespoons butter, soft
- 2 ¼ teaspoons instant yeast
- 1 teaspoon vanilla
- ½ teaspoon salt
- ½ teaspoon almond extract

Glaze

- 1 ¼ cups powdered sugar
- 3 tablespoons milk
- 1 teaspoon vanilla extract
- ½ teaspoon almond extract

Preparation instructions:

1. Make the dough the night before. In a large bowl, mix flour, sugar, yeast and salt together. Beat in milk, butter, extracts and egg till dough forms.
2. Transfer dough to a lightly floured surface and knead about 6 minutes. Place the dough into a buttered bowl and cover with plastic. Chill overnight.
3. Next day, transfer dough to a well-floured work surface. Press into a rectangle about 12 x 8 inches. Sprinkle the cherries over the dough being sure to leave about ½ inch at the edges plain. Roll up along the widest side. Slice into 12 pieces, place on flour dusted, line cookie sheet and loosely cover. Let rise for 20-30 minutes or till double in size.
4. Lightly spray the rolls with cooking spray, then add 2 at a time to the fryer basket. Place in the cooker and secure the Tender Crisp lid. Set the temperature for 360 degrees and cook 1 -2 minutes on each side, or till they are golden brown. Remove to a wire rack and repeat with remaining rolls.
5. Whisk the glaze ingredients together in a medium bowl. Dip the top of each fritter in glaze then place back on the rack. Allow several minutes for the glaze to set before serving.

Double Meat Breakfast Casserole

This hearty breakfast casserole features both bacon and sausage. The red and green peppers also give it a festive look so it would be ideal to serve for a holiday brunch or breakfast.

Yields: 4 -6 servings

Prep Time: 10 minutes

Cook Time: 50 minutes

Ingredients:

- ½ pound breakfast sausage
- 2 cups hash browns, shredded and thawed
- 4 slices bacon, chopped
- 6 eggs
- ¾ cup Velveeta, cubed
- ½ cup cheddar cheese, grated
- ½ cup mushrooms, sliced
- ¼ cup red bell pepper, chopped
- ¼ cup green bell pepper, chopped
- ¼ cup onion, chopped fine
- 2 -3 tablespoons sour cream

Preparation instructions:

1. Set the cooker to saute on med-high heat. Add the sausage and cook till brown. Remove with a slotted spoon and set aside.
2. Add bacon and cook, the remove it and set aside too. Drain all but 2 tablespoons of fat from the cooking pot.
3. Add vegetables and hash browns to the pot and cook till vegetables soften, stirring often. Stir in Velveeta cheese and continue cooking till it is melted and combined.
4. Meanwhile, in a large mixing bowl, whisk together eggs, sour cream, cheddar cheese and cooked bacon together.
5. Once the Velveeta is melted, top with sausage then pour the egg mixture over that.
6. Lock the Tender Crisp lid in place and set the temperature to 350 degrees. Bake the casserole for 35 -40 minutes or the center is set. Let rest 10 minutes before serving.

Easy Glazed Doughnuts

Doughnuts are irresistible to just about everybody. Now, your Ninja Foodi makes it super simple to make them at home. Let the kids help by cutting out the dough and decorating them with their favorite sprinkles.

Yields: 8 doughnuts & 8 doughnut holes
Prep Time: 1 hour
Cook Time: 5 mins
Ingredients:

- 2 cups flour
- ½ cup milk, room temperature
- ¼ cup sugar
- 1 egg, beaten
- 2 tablespoons butter, melted
- 1 ½ teaspoons fast acting yeast
- ¼ teaspoon nutmeg, optional
- salt

Glaze:

- 1 cup powdered sugar
- 4 teaspoons water
- candy sprinkles

Preparation instructions:

1. Combine dry ingredients in a large bowl. Stir in milk, butter and egg to form a soft dough.
2. Transfer dough to a lightly floured surface and knead 2-3 minutes till smooth. Place the dough in a lightly oiled bowl, cover and let rise in a warm place till double in size, about 30 minutes.
3. Turn dough out onto a lightly floured surface and roll out to 1/4-inch thickness. Cut out 8 doughnuts using a 3-inch round cutter. Then use a 1-inch round cutter to remove center.
4. Leave the doughnuts and holes on the lightly floured surface and loosely cover with a cloth, let rise till double again.
5. Lightly spray the basket with cooking spray. Place half the doughnuts in the basket, in a single layer. Secure the Tender Crisp lid and set the temperature to 350 degrees. Cook 4 -5 minutes till golden brown. Repeat
6. To make the glaze, whisk the powdered sugar and water together till thoroughly mixed. Dip the doughnuts and holes in the glaze and place on a wire rack. Top with candy sprinkles. Let set about 10 minutes, till glaze hardens, then serve.

Eggs Benedict Bread Pudding

If you love the flavors of eggs Benedict, then you will adore this bread pudding version. It has all the same flavors, eggs, English muffins, Canadian bacon, asparagus and Hollandaise just served up with a whole new look.

Yields: 4 – 6 servings

Prep Time: 15 minutes

Cook Time: 90 minutes

Ingredients:

- ½ pound Canadian bacon, cubed
- 4 asparagus spears, ends trimmed and cut into ½ inch pieces
- 3 English muffins, separated and cut into quarters
- 1 ½ cups milk
- 1 ½ cups half-and-half
- 6 eggs
- 1 package Hollandaise sauce mix
- 2 tablespoons fresh chives, chopped fine
- 1 teaspoon salt
- ¾ teaspoon white pepper

For the Hollandaise Sauce

- ¾ cup butter, cubed
- 3 large egg yolks
- 1 ½ teaspoons fresh lemon juice
- ½ teaspoon salt
- Pinch of white pepper
- Pinch of cayenne

Preparation instructions:

1. Make the main part of the dish the night before serving. Heat oven to 375 degrees.
2. Place muffin pieces on a baking sheet and cook for 10 – 12 minutes or till toasted and crunchy.

3. Set the cooker to sauté on med-high heat. Add bacon and cook till lightly browned. Add in asparagus and cook, stirring often, about 4 minutes. Add toasted muffin pieces to bacon mix and toss well.

4. In a large mixing bowl, whisk together sauce mix packet and milk. Add eggs, half-and-half, salt, and pepper and whisk till thoroughly combined. Add the bacon mixture and stir well. Cover with foil and refrigerate 6 hours or overnight.

5. In the morning, remove the pudding mix from the fridge and let come to room temperature.

6. Lightly spray the cooking pot with cooking spray and attach the Tender Crisp lid. Transfer the egg mixture to the cooking pot and top with chives. Secure the lid and set temperature to 350 degrees. Bake for 45 minutes or it passes the toothpick test.

7. While it is baking prepare the Hollandaise sauce: place the butter in a saucepan over medium heat and melt till frothy, but not boiling.

8. Place remaining ingredients in a blender and process till combined. Keep the blender running as you slowly add the melted butter. The sauce will thicken, it is best to make the sauce during the last 10 minutes of baking time.

9. To serve, cut the bread pudding into wedges and top with the sauce. Enjoy.

French Toast & Cream Cheese Casserole

This takes your basic French toast to whole new heights. Layered flavors of cream cheese, vanilla and cinnamon topped with a sweet, crunchy topping. It is ideal for a weekend breakfast or brunch. You can add some fresh fruit or sprinkle it with powdered sugar before serving to dress it up even more.

Yields: 4 - 6 servings
Prep Time: 15 minutes
Cook Time: 45 minutes
Ingredients:

- 1 small loaf of bread, sourdough or challah is ideal
- 1 cup milk
- 4 eggs
- ½ cup cream cheese, soft
- ½ cup brown sugar, packed
- 1 tablespoon powdered sugar
- 1 ½ teaspoons vanilla, divided
- ½ teaspoon cinnamon

Streusel Topping

- ¼ cup brown sugar
- ¼ cup flour
- 3 tablespoons butter, cold and cubed
- ½ teaspoon cinnamon

Preparation instructions:

1. Lightly spray cooking pot with cooking spray.
2. Slice the bread then cut it into 1-inch cubed. Layer half of them in the prepared cooking pot.
3. In a mixing bowl, beat the cream cheese till smooth. Add powdered sugar and ¼ teaspoon of the vanilla and mix till combined. Drop by spoonful's on top of the bread. Add remaining bread cubes.
4. In a separate bowl, whisk together eggs, milk, cinnamon, brown sugar and remaining vanilla till combined and no lumps remain. Pour over the bread. Cover tightly with plastic wrap and refrigerate 3 hours or overnight.
5. Before baking, remove from refrigerator and prepare the topping: In a small bowl, stir together the dry ingredients. Cut in butter with a pastry knife or two forks. Sprinkle over the bread mixture.
6. Place the pot in the cooker and secure the Tender Crisp lid. Set the temperature to 350 degrees and bake for 45 minutes or golden brown on top. Serve it while warm with fruit or syrup.

Maple Sausage Bread Pudding

This delicious breakfast recipe tastes like pancakes and sausage drizzled with maple syrup. It goes together quickly and disappears even faster. It makes a tasty treat for those chilly autumn mornings or on the holidays.

Yields: 4 -6 servings

Prep Time: 10 minutes

Cooking Time: 7 -8 hours

Ingredients:

- 1 pound sausage, casings removed
- 1 small baguette, cubed
- 2 cups milk
- 1 ½ cups cheddar cheese, cubed
- ½ cup heavy cream
- ½ cup maple syrup
- 4 eggs

Preparation instructions:

1. Set cooker to sauté on med heat and add sausage. Cook, breaking it up into bite-size pieces, do not crumble it. Transfer to strainer and drain off fat. Cool completely.
2. In a large mixing bowl, whisk together eggs, milk, cream and syrup till smooth. Add the bread pieces, sausage and cheese and stir to combine, most of the liquid should soak into the bread.
3. Set the cooker to slow cooking function on low heat. Secure the lid and cook 7 -8 hours, or overnight. Serve warm drizzled with more maple syrup.

Sausage and Spinach Breakfast Casserole

This hearty, healthy breakfast is a great way to start the day. Sausage, eggs, potatoes, spinach and Swiss cheese all cook overnight, so all you have to do is serve it up in the morning.

Yields: 6 -8 servings

Prep Time: 10 minutes

Cook Time: 6 – 8 hours

Ingredients:

- 1 pound breakfast sausage, casings removed
- 5 cups baby spinach, packed
- 1 bag of O'Brien potatoes, frozen
- 2 cups milk
- 8 eggs
- 1 ¼ cups Swiss cheese, grated
- 1 small onion, chopped fine
- ¼ cup Parmesan cheese, grated
- 2 teaspoons Dijon mustard
- 1 ½ teaspoons oregano
- 1 ½ teaspoons salt
- ¼ teaspoon freshly ground black pepper
- Red pepper flakes or hot sauce, for serving

Preparation instructions:

1. Set cooker to sauté on med-high heat. Add sausage, onion, and oregano and cook, breaking up the sausage till no longer pink, about 8 minutes. Add spinach and stir till wilted. Drain off the excess fat.
2. Add potatoes, 1 cup Swiss cheese, and the Parmesan cheese and stir to combine.
3. In a large bowl, whisk eggs, milk, mustard, salt and pepper together. Pour over sausage mix making sure you have an even layer.
4. Secure the lid and select slow cooker function on low heat. Cook 6 -8 hours or till the eggs are set. Top with remaining Swiss cheese and replace lid till it melts. Serve with pepper flakes or hot sauce if you like.

Strawberries & Cream Quinoa

Here is new take on a hot and hearty breakfast. Ditch the oatmeal and serve up a delicious, healthy quinoa instead. Best part is, this is gluten free and lower in fat that ordinary oatmeal, and you can cook it overnight and get up to a warm breakfast that is ready when you are.

Yields: 3-4 servings

Prep Time: 5 minutes

Cook Time: 8 hours

Ingredients:

- 2 cups milk
- 1 ½ cups strawberries, halved
- 1 cup dry quinoa, rinsed
- 1 medium banana, sliced
- 2 tablespoons butter
- Honey to taste

Preparation instructions:

1. Add all ingredients to cooking pot and stir to combine.
2. Secure the lid and select slow cooking function on low heat. Cook 6 – 8 hours.
3. Serve warm topped with honey.

Walnut Date Oatmeal

One of the joys of using a pressure cooker is that you can cut most cooking times in half. That is perfect when you need to get breakfast on the table on those busy week day mornings. This tasty oatmeal combines the rich flavors of walnuts and dates, but you could substitute other fruits and nuts according to the season.

Yields: 2-3 servings

Prep Time: 5 minutes

Cook Time: 3 minutes

Ingredients:

- 2 ¼ cups water
- 1 cup old-fashioned rolled oats
- 2 tablespoons walnuts, chopped
- 2 tablespoons dates, pitted and chopped
- ½ banana, sliced

Preparation instructions:

1. Add all ingredients to the cooking pot.
2. Secure lid and select pressure cooker setting with high pressure. Set timer for 3 minutes. When timer goes off use quick release to remove the lid. Stir and serve drizzled with honey or brown sugar.

MAIN DISHES

Baked Calamari & Shrimp Pasta

Calamari and shrimp marinated in rum then baked with pasta and spices, delicious. This dish goes together quickly and is sure to impress your friends and family.

Yields: 4 servings

Prep Time: 15 mins

Cook Time: 45 mins

Ingredients:

- 1 squid, cut into rings
- ½ pound shrimp, deveined and peeled
- 3 cups milk
- 2 cups mushrooms, sliced
- 1 ½ cups mozzarella cheese, grated
- 1 ¼ cups pasta, cooked
- 4 cloves garlic, chopped fine
- 3 tablespoons butter
- 3 tablespoons flour
- 2 tablespoons olive oil
- 2 teaspoons white rum
- ½ teaspoon thyme
- ¼ teaspoon chicken bouillon
- ¼ teaspoon nutmeg
- sea salt and pepper to taste

Preparation instructions:

1. In a small bowl, add shrimp and 1 teaspoon rum, salt and pepper and mix well.
2. In another small bowl, repeat with the squid.
3. Set the cooker to sauté on med-high heat and add 1 tablespoon of the oil. Once the oil is warm add the garlic and cook till fragrant, about 1 minute. Add mushrooms and cook, stirring often, till they are cooked through and no liquid remains. Transfer to a plate or bowl and set aside.

4. Add ½ tablespoon of oil to the cooking pot and cook shrimp till both sides are pink but they are not cooked through. Remove to bowl and set aside.

5. Add the remaining oil and squid and cook till it turns white but is not cooked through. Remove to bowl and set aside.

6. Turn the temperature down to med-low and add butter. Once the butter is melted, whisk in flour till completely combined. Cook and stir for about 2 minutes before adding milk. Stir while turning the heat up to med and continue to cook till mixture is boiling. Turn the heat back to med-low and stir in salt, pepper, bouillon, thyme and nutmeg. Simmer about 5 minutes, or sauce thickens.

7. Turn off the sauté function. Stir the pasta into the sauce. Top with a layer of shrimp, then the calamari, the mushrooms and finally the mozzarella. Secure the Tender Crisp lid and select bake at 350 degrees.

8. Cook the casserole 15 – 20 minutes, or till heated through and cheese is melted and browned. Serve.

Beer Braised Brisket

This tender beef brisket is cooked in Mexican beer with onion and spices. Serve it with warm flour tortillas and refried beans. You can also substitute the Mexican beer with a domestic one and use the shredded beef for sandwiches or as a main dish with your favorite side.

Yields: 8 – 10 servings

Prep Time: 10 minutes

Cook Time: 8 hours

Ingredients:

- 5 pound beef brisket
- 1 large can tomatoes, diced
- 1 bottle of Modelo beer
- 1 medium onion, sliced thin
- 3 cloves garlic, chopped fine
- 1 tablespoon plus 1 teaspoon oregano
- 1 tablespoon salt
- 1 tablespoon freshly ground black pepper

Preparation instructions:

1. Place the onion on the bottom of the cooking pot. Add brisket, fat side up, if you need to cut it into pieces to fit the pot then that is okay. Add the tomatoes, undrained and beer. Sprinkle the garlic and seasonings on the top.

2. Secure the lid and select the slow cooker function on low heat. Cook 8 hours, or till beef is fork tender.

3. Carefully transfer the brisket to a cutting board and slice or shred it. Return it to the pot and stir before serving.

Cheesy Shepherd's Pie

This is comfort food at its best. Since it is cooked with the pressure cooker setting, you can have it on the table in no time. If you want a nice, melted, bubble cheese topping, just pop on the Tender Crisp lid after cooking and broil it to your desired doneness.

Yields: 6 servings

Prep Time: 10 minutes

Cook Time: 30 minutes

Ingredients:

- 1 pound ground beef
- 3 medium russet potatoes, peeled and cut into 1-inch cubes
- 3 carrot, chopped
- 1 cup onion, chopped fine
- 1 cup mushrooms, chopped
- 1 cup peas, frozen
- 1 cup water
- 1 cup beef broth
- 1 cup cheddar cheese, grated
- 1 egg
- 2 tablespoons butter
- 2 tablespoons Worcestershire
- 2 tablespoons flour
- 1 ½ teaspoons salt
- 1 teaspoon garlic powder
- 1 teaspoon pepper

Preparation instructions:

1. Add potatoes and water to cooking pot. Secure lid and select pressure cooking on high. Set timer for 8 minutes. When the timer goes off, drain the potatoes and place them in a large mixing bowl.

2. Add the egg, garlic powder, ½ teaspoon salt and butter and blend together with a hand mixer. Set aside.

3. Set the cooker to sauté on med-high heat and add the ground beef. Cook, stirring often, till no longer pink. Drain the grease. Add Worcestershire, vegetables, salt and pepper and stir to combine.

4. In a small measuring cup, stir the flour and broth together then add to beef mixture. Cook, stirring often, about 3 minutes or till sauce begins to thicken. Transfer to a baking dish that will fit inside the cooking pot.

5. Top the beef mixture with the mashed potatoes in an even layer. Cover the dish with foil.

6. Rinse out the cooking pot and add the rack to it. Add ½ cups water then place the baking dish on the rack. Secure the lid and select pressure cooking on high. Set the timer for 10 minutes.

7. Use quick release to remove the lid. Carefully remove the dish from the pot, unless you are going to broil the top. Remove the foil and sprinkle the cheese on top. Let rest for 10 minutes before serving.

Chicken Poblano

This tasty, Mexican flavored chicken is a versatile dish that allows you to serve it in a number of ways. It makes a great filling for tacos, burritos or enchiladas. Or just serve it with Mexican rice, refried beans and some warm tortillas.

Yields: 4 servings

Prep Time: 10 minutes

Cook Time: 3 hours

Ingredients:

- 1 package chicken thighs, boneless and skinless
- 3 Poblano chilies, seeded and sliced thin
- 1 cup onions, sliced thin
- ½ cup heavy whipping cream
- 3 cloves garlic, chopped fine
- 3 tablespoons taco seasoning
- 2 tablespoons olive oil
- ½ teaspoon salt
- ¼ teaspoon ground black pepper

Preparation instructions:

1. Set the cooker to sauté on med-high heat. Add 1 tablespoon of the oil and heat. Add chilies, onions and garlic and cook, stirring often, 6-7 minutes, till tender crisp. Remove and set aside.

2. Heat the remaining oil and add chicken. Cook 4-5 minutes, till browned on the outside.

3. Select slow cooker function on low heat. Add the onion mix to the chicken along with the seasoning, salt and pepper. Stir to combine.

4. Secure the lid and cook 2-3 hours, or chicken is cooked through. Stir in the cream and cook another 15 minutes. Stir before serving.

Chicken Potato & Broccoli Casserole

The combination of chicken, potatoes, bacon and cheese is so tasty the kids won't even mind that there is broccoli here too! A few simple steps and you can serve up a healthy, balanced meal they will want more of.

Yields: 6 -8 servings

Prep Time: 10 minutes

Cook Time: 40 minutes

Ingredients:

- 3 pounds red potatoes, cut into 1-inch pieces
- 3 cups chicken, cooked and chopped
- 2-3 cups broccoli florets
- 4 slices bacon, cooked and crumbled
- 2 cups cheddar cheese, grated
- 1 cup sour cream
- 4 tablespoons butter, soft
- 1 teaspoon salt
- ½ teaspoon freshly ground black pepper
- ½ teaspoon garlic powder
- ½ teaspoon paprika

Preparation instructions:

1. Place the potatoes and 1 cup of water in the cooking pot. Secure the lid and select pressure cooking on high. Cook the potatoes 8 minutes. Use quick release and drain the potatoes. Mash them and set aside.
2. Place the broccoli and 1 cup of water in the pot and repeat above, cooking the broccoli for 3 minutes. Drain and set aside.
3. Lightly spray the cooking pot with cooking spray. Add the mashed potatoes to the hot pot and stir in the butter, sour cream and seasonings. Stir to combine.
4. Add the broccoli, bacon, chicken and half the cheese. Stir to mix well. Sprinkle the remaining cheese on top.
5. Switch to the Tender Crisp lid and set to 350 degrees. Bake 20 – 25 minutes, or till the casserole is heated through and the cheese has melted. Serve.

Chipotle Chicken Bowls

This delicious Mexican dish almost takes more time to prepare than it does to cook! Serve it with warm flour tortillas, guacamole and your favorite salsa for an easy week night meal.

Yields: 4 servings

Prep Time: 10 minutes

Cook Time: 6 minutes

Ingredients:

- 1 pound chicken, boneless, skinless and cut into bite sized pieces
- 4 cups tomatoes, diced in juice
- 1 can black beans, drain and rinse
- 1 small onion, chopped
- 1 cup jasmine rice, uncooked
- ½ cup water
- ½ lime, juiced
- 2 tablespoons butter
- 1 tablespoon chipotle peppers in adobo, pureed
- 2 teaspoons salt
- ½ teaspoon black pepper

Preparation instructions:

1. Place all ingredients, except the beans, into the cooking pot. Stir to combine.
2. Secure the lid and select pressure cooking on high. Set timer for 6 minutes. When the timer goes off, use quick release to remove the lid.
3. Stir in the beans and serve.

Crab Frittata

This light and fluffy frittata cooks up quickly in your Ninja Foodi. It is ideal for a light lunch, or serve with a crisp salad and toasty bread for an easy summer dinner. Heck, you could even eat it for breakfast if you wanted to.

Yields: 4 servings

Prep Time: 10 mins

Cook Time: 50 mins

Ingredients:

- 2 cups lump crabmeat
- 4 eggs
- 1 cup half and half
- 1 cup Parmesan cheese, grated
- 1 cup green onions, chopped
- 1 teaspoon salt
- 1 teaspoon pepper
- 1 teaspoon sweet smoked paprika
- 1 teaspoon Italian seasoning

Preparation instructions:

1. Whisk egg and half-and-half together in a large bowl. Add seasonings and Parmesan and stir to mix.
2. Stir in the onions and crab meat.
3. Wrap some foil around the base of a springform pan that will fit inside the cooking pot. Pour the egg mixture into the pan.
4. Place the rack in the pot and add 2 cups of water. Place the pan on the rack and secure the lid. Select pressure cooking on high and set the timer for 40 minutes.
5. When the timer goes off, let sit for 10 minutes. Then use quick release to remove the lid. Carefully remove the pan and remove the outer ring. Serve warm or at room temperature.

Creamy Braised Oxtails

These tender, braised oxtails have just a touch of Asian flavor in a creamy sauce. Serve them over rice or noodles with your favorite vegetable for a hearty meal.

Yields: 6 servings

Prep Time: 10 mins

Cook Time: 1 hour 5 mins

Ingredients:

- 2 pounds oxtails
- 1 onion, chopped
- 1 cup beef broth
- ½ cup heavy cream
- ¼ cup sake
- 4 cloves garlic, chopped
- 2 tablespoons chili bean sauce
- 1 teaspoon Chinese five spice
- 1 teaspoon bacon fat, or butter
- Salt and pepper

Preparation instructions:

1. Set the cooker to sauté on medium heat and add bacon fat.
2. Sprinkle the oxtails with salt and pepper and brown on all sides, about 3-5 minutes each sides.
3. Add onion and garlic and continue cooking another 3-5 minutes. Add the sake to deglaze the pot and cook 1-2 minute to reduce the liquid.
4. Add the broth, chili bean sauce and five spice. Secure the lid and select the pressure cooking setting on high. Set the timer for 60 minutes. When the timer goes off, use the quick release to remove the lid.
5. Put it back on the sauté setting on low heat and bring the oxtails to a simmer. Add the cream and simmer about 5 minutes or till the sauce has thickened. Serve.

Duck Confit

The secret to getting all the flavor you can out of the duck is let it set in the refrigerator as long as possible. This is a delicious dish just as good as you would get in any restaurant.

Yields: 4 servings

Prep Time: 24 - 72 hours' curing time

Cook Time: 2 hours

Ingredients:

- 4 duck legs, drumsticks and thighs
- 4 sprigs fresh thyme
- 4 cloves garlic, smashed
- 2 bay leaves, halved
- 1 tablespoon salt
- ¼ teaspoon peppercorns, lightly crushed
- ¼ teaspoon allspice berries, lightly crushed

Preparation instructions:

1. Line a baking sheet with paper towels. Place all the spices, salt and pepper in a large mixing bowl and stir to combine. Add the duck legs and toss to coat evenly. Lay them in a single layer on the baking sheet and refrigerate at least 24 hours, or up to 3 days.. Do not cover.

2. Brush the garlic and thyme off the duck, set it aside for later. Set the cooker to sauté on med-high heat.

3. Add the duck legs and sear till golden brown on all sides and the fat starts to render, about 5 – 10 minutes per side. Scatter the reserved garlic and thyme over the duck.

4. Secure the lid and select pressure cooking on high. Set the timer for 40 minutes. Use manual release to remove the lid. Flip the legs over and cook another 30 minutes. Again use manual release to remove the lid.

5. Let it cool completely then cover the pot and refrigerate. When the liquid cools the fat will separate from the stock, save the stock for soups or other recipes for later.

6. When ready to serve, scrape the fat off the duck and lay it on a baking sheet. Broil it till the skin is crispy, about 3 – 5 minutes. Serve.

Easy Baked Beef & Pasta

All the delicious Italian flavor of a lasagna without all the work. This tasty casserole can be on the table in less than an hour! Serve it up with some toasty garlic bread and a tossed green salad.

Yields: 6 servings

Prep Time: 20 mins

Cook Time: 20 mins

Ingredients:

- 1 ½ pounds ground beef
- 28 ounce can tomatoes, crushed
- 2 cups Mozzarella cheese, grated
- 2 cups Fusilli pasta, cooked
- ½ cup onion, chopped
- ¼ cup Parmesan cheese, grated
- 4 teaspoons garlic, chopped fine
- 2 teaspoons oregano
- ¼ teaspoon red pepper flakes
- fresh parsley for garnish

Preparation instructions:

1. Set the cooker to sauté on medium heat. Add ground beef and cook till no longer pink. Stir in onion, garlic, oregano and red pepper flakes. Add salt and pepper to taste.

2. Stir in pasta, tomatoes and half the Mozzarella cheese. Sprinkle the remaining Mozzarella and the Parmesan over the top.

3. Add the Tender Crisp lid and set the temperature to 350 degrees. Bake for 20 minutes, or till heated through and cheese is golden brown. Serve with chopped fresh parsley sprinkled on the top.

Korean Chicken

This tasty chicken dish packs a punch of flavors. Serve it with, or without, the mango salsa (recipe included) over rice. Since it is slow cooked you can add the ingredients in the morning, then when you get home dinner is ready!

Yields: 6 servings

Prep Time: 15 minutes

Cook Time: 3 -4 hours

Ingredients:

- 2 pounds chicken thighs, boneless and skinless
- ¼ cup soy sauce
- ¼ cup honey
- 4 cloves garlic, chopped fine
- 2 tablespoons Korean chili paste
- 2 tablespoons toasted sesame oil
- 2 tablespoons fresh ginger, grated
- 2 teaspoons cornstarch
- Pinch of red pepper flakes

For the Mango Salsa:

- 2 ripe mangoes, peeled, pitted, and diced
- ¼ red onion, chopped fine
- Juice of 1 lime
- 1 jalapeno pepper, seeded and chopped fine
- 1 tablespoon cilantro, chopped
- Drizzle of honey
- Salt, to taste

Preparation instructions:

1. Add the soy sauce, honey, chili paste, sesame oil, ginger, garlic and pepper flakes to the cooking pot, stir to combine. Add the chicken and turn to coat in the sauce.
2. Secure the lid and select slow cooking function on low. Cook 3 – 4 hours or till chicken is cooked through.
3. While the chicken is cooking, make the salsa. Add the mango, jalapeno, onion and cilantro to a bowl. Juice the lime over the top and add honey to taste. Stir, cover and refrigerate till ready to serve.
4. When the chicken is cooked, transfer it to a plate. Set the cooker to sauté on med-low heat. Whisk the cornstarch into ¼ cup of cold water and add to the sauce. Cook, stirring constantly, about 5 minutes or till thick and glossy.
5. Shred the chicken and add it back to the sauce, stirring to coat. Serve with the salsa and garnish with sesame seeds or chopped scallions if desired.

Lamb Marsala

Tender lamb shanks braised in red wine with garlic and rosemary, yummy. Serve with mashed potatoes and your favorite green veggie for a restaurant worthy dinner that you made at home.

Yields: 2 servings

Prep Time: 5 minutes

Cook Time: 1 hour 40 minutes

Ingredients:

- 2 lamb shanks
- 1 cup chicken stock
- 2/3 cup Marsala wine
- 1 onion, chopped
- 8 cloves garlic, halved
- 4 bay leaves
- 2 tablespoons tomato paste
- 2 twigs rosemary
- Salt & pepper to taste
- Olive oil

Preparation instructions:

1. Trim off the excess fat from the lamb. Rub them with salt and pepper.
2. Set the cooker to sauté on med-high heat and add a splash of olive oil. When the oil is hot add the onions and garlic and cook till almost translucent, stirring often. Stir in the tomato paste and cook 2-3 minutes more.
3. Add lamb shanks, one at a time, and brown on both sides. Add both shanks to the pot, making sure they are meat side down. Add the bay leaves, wine, rosemary and chicken stock and bring to a boil.
4. Secure the lid and select pressure cooking on high. Set the timer for 45 minutes.
5. When the timer goes off, use quick release to remove the lid. Flip the lamb and secure the lid again. Cook another 25 minutes.
6. Quick release the lid and set the cooker back to sauté on medium heat. Cook another 10 – 15 minutes till the sauce is thick and sticky, being sure to glaze the lamb every few minutes. Serve.

Pork Loin with Onion Beer Sauce

Tender pork loin braised in a rich, onion beer sauce. And since it is cooked using the pressure cooker, it is done in less than an hour. Serve over egg noodles, or with mashed potatoes for a tasty meal.

Yields: 4 – 6 servings

Prep Time: 5 minutes

Cook Time: 40 minutes

Ingredients:

- 1 ½ pound pork loin
- 1 ½ cups dark beer
- 1 large onion, sliced
- 2 cloves garlic, chopped fine
- 3 tablespoons water
- 2 tablespoons cornstarch
- 1 tablespoon olive oil
- 1 tablespoon Dijon mustard
- 2 bay leaves

Preparation instructions:

1. Set cooker to sauté on medium heat and add oil. Once oil is hot, add onions and cook till tender. Add the pork loin and brown on all sides, transfer to a plate.
2. Add the beer and stir to deglaze the pan. Stir in the mustard, garlic and bay leaves and add the pork loin back to the pot.
3. Secure the lid and switch to pressure cooking on high. Set the timer for 35 minutes. When the timer goes off, use manual release to remove the lid.
4. Dissolve the cornstarch in the water. Remove the pork and set the cooker back to sauté on med-high heat. Add the cornstarch mixture to the pot and cook till sauce thickens.
5. Slice the pork and serve with the onion beer sauce.

Sausage Onions & Peppers

Easy sausage, onions and peppers can be served over rice, or used to make yummy sandwiches. To make sandwiches, serve on toasted hoagie rolls with some melted provolone on top.

Yields: 4 servings

Prep Time: 10 minutes

Cook Time: 4 hours

Ingredients:

- 1 pound Italian sausage, casings removed
- 1-2 cans tomatoes, diced
- 1 large onion, chopped
- 1 green pepper, seeded and chopped
- 3-4 cloves garlic, chopped fine
- ½ teaspoon salt

Preparation instructions:

1. Set cooker to sauté on med-high heat. Add sausage and brown, breaking up into large chunks.

2. Add remaining ingredients and secure the lid. Set to slow cooking on high and cook for 4 hours. Serve.

Seafood Casserole

This seafood casserole is creamy, cheesy and slightly spice all at the same time. The recipe calls for lump crabmeat but you could substitute imitation if you prefer. Serve this tasty dish with some toasted garlic bread for lunch or dinner.

Yields: 6 servings

Prep time: 20 mins

Cook time: 15 mins

Ingredients:

- 1 pound large shrimp, peeled and deveined
- 1 ½ cups ziti, cooked
- 1 cup lump crab meat
- 1 can chicken broth
- 1 cup sour cream
- ¾ cup Colby jack cheese, grated
- 1/3 cup sweet onion, chopped
- ¼ cup jalapenos, seeded and chopped
- ¼ cup flour
- 2 tablespoons butter
- 2 tablespoons sherry
- 2 cloves garlic, chopped fine
- ½ teaspoon Old Bay seasoning
- ¼ teaspoon white pepper
- Chopped cilantro for garnish

Preparation instructions:

1. Sprinkle the shrimp with the Old Bay seasoning and toss to coat.
2. Add butter to the cooking pot and set to sauté on med-low heat. When the butter melts, add onion, garlic and jalapenos and cook till tender, stirring often.
3. Add the seafood, sherry and broth and cook till shrimp are pink.
4. In a mixing bowl, whisk together the sour cream, pepper and flour. Add to seafood mixture and stir well. Reduce heat to low and cook till thickened.
5. Stir in the pasta then top with the cheese. Add the Tender Crisp lid and set the temperature to 350 degrees. Bake 10 – 15 minutes till heated through and cheese it bubbly and starts to brown. Serve garnished with chopped cilantro.

Speedy Paella

Paella is a traditional Spanish dish that it is usually cooked in a large, shallow pan. One of the best parts about the traditional dish is the crispy rice layer on the bottom. Now you can make an easier version of this tasty dish at home.

Yields: 6 servings

Prep Time: 20 minutes

Cook Time: 25 minutes

Ingredients:

- 1 pound Spanish chorizo, cut into ½-inch slices
- 1 pound shrimp, deveined but leave tails and shell on
- 1 pound Little neck clams, scrubbed
- 4 cups chicken broth
- 2 cups long grain rice
- 1 cup roasted red peppers, sliced
- 1 onion, chopped
- ½ cup green olives, pitted
- ½ cup dry white wine
- 3 cloves garlic, chopped fine
- 2 tablespoons olive oil
- 1 teaspoon smoked paprika
- ½ teaspoon saffron threads, crumbled
- Salt & pepper

Preparation instructions:

1. Set the cooker to sauté on med-high heat and add the oil. Once the oil is hot, add the chorizo and cook till browned on both sides, about 3 minutes. Transfer to a plate and set aside.

2. Add the onion and garlic and cook till translucent, about 3 – 4 minutes. Season with salt and pepper. Add the wine and deglaze the pan. Continue cooking till wine is reduced by half, about 2 minutes.

3. Add the rice, paprika and saffron and cook till rice is well coated, about 1 minute. Add the broth and a pinch of salt. Secure the lid and set to pressure cooking on high. Set the timer for 5 minutes.

4. Once the timer goes off, use quick release to remove the lid. Add the shrimp and clams to the pot. Cover and cook on high pressure for 6 minutes, or till shrimp are pink and clams have opened. Use quick release to remove the lid again.

5. Discard any unopened clams. Add the chorizo, olives and red peppers and stir to combine. Serve.

Southwest Short Ribs

This recipe for tender, southwest flavored short ribs, includes a colorful succotash to go with it. This meal uses the best of fall vegetables for a hearty meal everyone will enjoy.

Yields: 4-6 servings

Prep Time: 15 minutes

Cook Time: 45 minutes

Ingredients:

- 3 pounds beef short ribs, trim off fat
- 1 pound yams, peeled and cubed
- 14.5 ounce can tomatoes, diced
- 1 cup red onion, chopped
- 1 cup green beans, thawed
- 1 cup corn, thawed
- 1 cup beef stock
- 1 cup pale ale
- 4 cloves garlic, chopped fine
- 2 teaspoons olive oil
- 2 teaspoons cumin
- 1 teaspoon salt
- 1 teaspoon Ancho chili powder
- ½ teaspoon pepper
- ½ teaspoon coriander

Preparation instructions:

1. Add the oil to the cooking pot and set to sauté on med-high heat. Sprinkle the ribs with salt and pepper and cook, in batches, till brown on each side. Transfer to a plate and set aside. Drain all but 1 tablespoon fat.

2. Add the onions and garlic and cook 2 minutes, stirring often. Add the beef stock and ale and deglaze the pan.

3. Add the yam, tomatoes, cumin, chili powder and coriander and stir well. Place the ribs back in the pot and secure the lid. Set to pressure cooking on high. Set the timer for 35 minutes.

4. When the timer goes off, use the manual release to remove the lid. Use a slotted spoon to remove the ribs and vegetables, placing them in two separate serving bowls.

5. Set the cooker back to sauté on med-high heat and cook sauce till it reduces and is thickened. To serve, place 2 ribs on the succotash and drizzle with sauce.

Sweet & Spicy Balsamic Beef

This tender, tangy roast beef will quickly become one of your favorite comfort foods. Serve with mashed, or baked potatoes and your favorite steamed veggies for a delicious, healthy meal. Any left overs can be used for sandwiches the next day.

Yields: 6 – 8 servings

Prep Time: 5 minutes

Cook Time: 6 – 8 hours

Ingredients:

- 3-4 pound beef roast, boneless
- 1 can beef broth
- ½ onion, chopped fine
- ½ cup balsamic vinegar
- 5 cloves garlic, chopped fine
- 3 tablespoons honey
- 1 tablespoon soy sauce
- 1 tablespoon Worcestershire sauce
- 1 teaspoon red chili flakes

Preparation instructions:

1. Place all ingredients, except the roast, into the cooking pot. Stir well. Add roast and turn to coat.

2. Add the lid and select slow cooking on low and cook 6-8 hours. When the beef is done, remove to a plate and shred, using two forks. Add it back to the sauce and serve.

Thai Sweet Pork

Thai Sweet Pork is a popular dish at Thai restaurants and if you have ever tried it you know how yummy it is. Now make this dish at home. Serve it over rice garnished with crispy, caramelized onions. This is one of these dishes that will impress the family!

Yields: 6 servings

Prep Time: 5 minutes

Cook Time: 15 minutes

Ingredients:

- 2 pounds pork shoulder, cut into ¼" x 2" strips
- 3 large shallots, sliced not too thin
- ¼ cup brown sugar
- ¼ cup palm sugar
- 3 cloves garlic, chopped fine
- 3 tablespoons soy sauce
- 2 tablespoons vegetable oil
- 2 tablespoons sweet soy sauce
- 2 tablespoons fish sauce
- 1 teaspoon ground chili paste
- ¼ teaspoon white pepper

Rice

- 1 ½ cups Jasmine rice, rinsed
- 1 can coconut milk
- ¼ cup water
- 1 teaspoon salt

Preparation instructions:

1. Set cooker to sauté on med-high heat. Add oil and shallots and cook two minutes. Add garlic and cook another 30 seconds.
2. Add soy sauce, fish sauce, chili paste, pepper and half the sugars and simmer 3 minutes.
3. Add the pork and stir to coat.
4. Place the rack in the pot and place a pan on top. Add the rice ingredients and cover with foil, poke holes in the foil to vent.
5. Secure the lid and set to pressure cooking on high. Set timer for 6 minutes. When timer goes off, use manual release to remove the lid.
6. Remove the pan of rice and set aside. Stir in the remaining sugars and set the cooker back to sauté on medium heat. Cook the sauce, stirring often, till it has thickened. Serve the pork over the rice garnished with chopped scallions and crispy, caramelized onions.

Veal Marengo

This classic French dish normally takes a while to cook, but on the pressure cooking function, you can have it on the table in just 30 minutes. Tender veal with vegetables that are braised in white wine, another dish sure to impress.

Yields: 8 servings
Prep Time: 10 minutes
Cook Time: 20 minutes

Ingredients:

- 4 pounds lean veal, cubed
- 1 pound mushrooms, quartered
- 1 ½ cups chicken broth
- 1 cup plus 2 tablespoons dry white wine
- 1 cup onion, chopped
- 1 cup celery, chopped
- 1 cup tomato sauce
- 2 long strips orange zest
- 2 sprigs fresh parsley
- 4 tablespoons light olive oil
- 2 tablespoons butter
- 2 tablespoons fresh lemon juice
- 2 teaspoons cornstarch
- 1 teaspoon garlic, chopped fine
- ½ teaspoon thyme
- Salt & pepper
- Chopped parsley for garnish

Preparation instructions:

1. Pat veal dry with paper towel and sprinkle with salt and pepper.
2. Add 2 tablespoons olive oil to the cooking pot and set to sauté on med-high heat. Working in batches, brown meat on all sides and transfer to a plate.
3. Add remaining oil to the pot along with onion, garlic and celery. Cook, stirring often, about 5 minutes or onion is tender. Add zest, bay leaf, thyme, broth and 1 cup wine. Bring to a boil and simmer 1 minute.
4. Add the veal back to the pot with the tomato sauce. Top with parsley sprigs, do not stir.
5. Secure the lid and select pressure cooking on high. Set the timer for 20 minutes. When the timer goes off, use quick release to remove the lid. Use a slotted spoon to remove the veal. Discard the bay leaf and orange zest.
6. Use an immersion blender to puree the sauce and season with salt if needed.
7. In a small mixing bowl, whisk the cornstarch and 2 tablespoons wine together. Stir into the sauce to thicken.
8. In a large skillet, over med-high heat, melt the butter. Add the mushrooms and lemon juice and cook till mushrooms soften, about 3-4 minutes. Add to the sauce along with the veal. Serve garnished with chopped parsley.

SIDE DISHES

Baked Beans

Delicious, easy to make baked beans perfect for backyard BBQ's or potlucks. The great thing about using a pressure cooker is you can skip the overnight soak and be ready to cook the beans in just one hour.

Yields: 10 servings
Prep Time: 1 hour
Cook Time: 40 minutes
Ingredients:

- 1 pound dried navy beans, rinsed
- ½ pound bacon, cut into 3-inch pieces
- 2 ½ cups water
- 1 cup onion, chopped
- ½ cup ketchup
- ¼ cup brown sugar
- 2 tablespoons molasses
- 1 teaspoon dry mustard
- ½ teaspoon salt
- ¼ teaspoon pepper

Preparation instructions:

1. Add beans to the cooking pot with enough water to cover them completely. Secure the lid and select pressure cooking on high. Cook for 1 minute, then let rest for one hour. Drain and rinse the beans and discard any that are floating.
2. Set the cooker to sauté on med-high heat. Add the bacon and cook till crisp. Transfer the bacon to a paper towel lined plate and set aside.
3. Add the onion and cook till tender, scraping up the brown bits on the bottom of the pot.
4. Add all of the ingredients, except the bacon to the onions and stir to combine. Set the cooker back to pressure cooking on high and cook 35 minutes.
5. When the timer goes off wait 10 minutes, then use quick release to remove the lid. Check to see if the beans are tender, if not cook a few minutes longer.
6. Set the cooker back to sauté on medium heat and stir in the bacon. Cook, stirring often, till sauce thickens to desired consistency. Serve or store in the refrigerator.

Braised Artichokes

The garlic, thyme and lemon used to braise the artichokes helps to bring out their natural flavor. By using the pressure cooking function you can have them ready for dinner in no time.

Yields: 6 servings

Prep Time: 25 minutes

Cook Time: 29 minutes

Ingredients:

- 6 large artichokes, stems peeled, outer leaves removed and halved
- 2 lemons, quartered
- 4-6 cloves garlic, crushed
- 4 thyme sprigs
- ½ cup extra-virgin olive oil
- Salt and freshly ground pepper, to taste

Preparation instructions:

1. Fill a large bowl with cold water and squeeze the juice from the quarters of one lemon into it. As you are prepping the artichokes, drop them in the bowl to prevent discoloration. Make sure to remove the furry choke and cut 1 inch off the top. Just before cooking, drain the artichokes and pat dry with paper towels.

2. Set cooker to sauté on med-high heat. Add the oil. Sprinkle the cut sides of the artichokes with salt and pepper. Working in batches, lay them cut side down in the pot and cook till browned, about 6 – 10 minutes.

3. Place all of the artichokes back in the pot along with remaining ingrediets. Secure the lid and select pressure cooking on high. Set the timer for 9 minutes. When the timer goes off, use quick release to remove the lid.

4. Transfer the artichokes to a serving bowl and squeeze the juice of the cooked lemons over them. Serve.

Carrot Pudding

This recipe takes the humble carrot to new heights. It is warm, rich and delicious and makes the perfect side dish for roast beef or pork, or save it for the holidays.

Yields: 4 servings

Prep Time: 10 minutes

Cook Time: 2 – 4 hours

Ingredients:

- 4 cups carrots, grated
- 1 small onion, grated
- 1 cup heavy cream
- 1 egg, beaten
- 1 tablespoon sugar
- 1 teaspoons salt
- 1 teaspoon nutmeg

Preparation instructions:

1. Place the carrots and onion in the cooking pot.
2. Whisk the remaining ingredients together in a mixing bowl, then pour over vegetables. Secure the lid and select slow cooking function. If using low heat, set the timer for 4 hours, or two hours on high.
3. When the timer goes off check to see if the carrots are tender. If not, cook a while longer. When the carrots are done, use an immersion blender, and pulse till the mixture resembles pudding. Serve warm.

Cheesy Green Chili Rice

This is a yummy side dish that pairs well with Mexican food or the Poblano Chicken in the previous chapter. Since it uses Anaheim chilies, and not jalapenos, it is not too spicy for the kids.

Yields: 6 – 8 servings

Prep Time: 25 minutes

Cook Time: 1 -2 hours

Ingredients:

- 4-5 cups long-grain white rice, cooked
- 2 cans green chilies, diced
- 2 cups scallions, sliced thin
- 1 ½ cups plus 3 tablespoons Mozzarella cheese, grated
- 1 cup sour cream
- 2 tablespoons Parmesan cheese
- 1-2 tablespoons green hot sauce

Preparation instructions:

1. Place the rice and scallions in a large bowl and stir together.
2. In a separate bowl, combine sour cream, chilies with their juice, hot sauce and 1 ½ cups of the Mozzarella cheese.
3. Mix the cheese mixture into the rice.
4. Lightly spray the cooking pot with cooking spray. Add the rice mixture and press down to make sure it is in an even layer. Top with remaining Mozzarella and the Parmesan cheese.
5. Secure the lid and select slow cooking on high heat. Cook 1-2 hours or till bubbling hot and cheese is melted. Serve.

Creamy Cheesy Polenta

This recipe lets you create creamy, perfect polenta with no worries, or lumps. Serve with your favorite beef or pork dishes along with a nice green vegetable for a hearty, satisfying meal.

Yields: 4 servings

Prep Time: 5 mins

Cook Time: 4 hrs

Ingredients:

- 3 cups vegetable broth
- 1 cup coarse cornmeal
- 1 cup half and half
- ¼ cup cheese, grated

Preparation instructions:

1. Combine the broth and cornmeal in the cooking pot. Secure the lid and select slow cooking on low heat. Cook 3 -4 hours, being sure to stir it every 30 minutes.

2. Add the half-and-half, stir well and turn the heat up to high and cook another 30 minutes. Stir in the cheese till melted. Serve.

Holiday Brussels Sprouts with Nuts & Cranberries

This tasty side dish combine Brussels sprouts with butternut squash, pecan and cranberries. It makes a festive dish for your holiday dinners and since it uses the slow cooker, it is hassle free.

Yields: 8 servings

Prep Time: 20 mins

Cook Time: 2 hours 30 mins

Ingredients:

- 4 cups Brussels sprouts, halved
- 4 cups butternut squash, cut into 1-inch cubes
- 1 red onion, cut into large chunks
- 1 cup cranberries
- ½ cup pecans

Maple Cinnamon Sauce

- ¼ cup maple syrup
- 2 tablespoons apple cider vinegar
- 1 teaspoon cinnamon
- ½ teaspoon salt
- ¼ teaspoon nutmeg

Preparation instructions:

1. Add the Brussels sprouts, squash and onion to the cooking pot and toss together. Secure the lid and select slow cooking on high. Cook 2 – 2 ½ hours, stirring every hour.

2. After 2 hours check for doneness, sprouts should be tender-crisp and squash should be tender without being mushy.

3. In a small saucepan, stir the sauce ingredients together over med-high heat. Bring to a boil, reduce heat and simmer, stirring often, 5 minutes, or till thickened

4. Just before serving add the cranberries to the vegetables in the pot and cook another 5 minutes.

5. To serve, transfer vegetables to a serving bowl and pour the sauce over, toss to coat. Top with pecans.

Lemon Orzo with Asparagus

This side dish combines orzo pasta and asparagus, all wrapped up in a buttery, lemon, cheesy sauce. It is packed with flavor and super simple to make.

Yields: 6 servings

Prep time: 10 mins

Cook time: 5 mins

Ingredients:

- 1 pound asparagus, tips only
- 3 cups water
- 1 cup orzo pasta, uncooked
- ¾ cup Parmesan cheese
- ¼ cup butter
- 2-3 tablespoons fresh lemon juice
- 2 tablespoons garlic, chopped fine
- salt and pepper to taste

Preparation instructions:

1. Cook pasta according to package directions, adding asparagus during the last 3 minutes of cooking. Drain.

2. Set cooker to sauté on medium heat. Add butter and let melt. Add the garlic and cook, stirring often, 2 minutes. Turn off the heat and stir in lemon juice and cheese. Add pasta and toss to coat. Serve immediately.

Pumpkin & Bacon Risotto

This creamy pumpkin risotto makes the perfect side dish for holiday dinners. And who doesn't love, cheesy risotto, pumpkin and bacon?

Yields: 6 servings

Prep Time: 20 min

Cook Time: 1 hour

Ingredients:

- 4 ½ cups chicken broth
- 6 strips bacon, chopped
- 1 ½ cups onion, chopped
- 1 cup Arborio rice, uncooked
- ½ cup Parmesan cheese
- ¼ cup pumpkin puree
- 2 tablespoons parsley, chopped
- 1 tablespoon olive oil
- salt and black pepper

Preparation instructions:

1. Set cooker to sauté on med-high heat and add oil. When the oil is hot, add bacon and onions and cook till onions are tender and bacon starts to crisp, about 15 minutes.

2. Add the rice, salt and pepper. Cook, stirring often, 5 minutes. Stir in broth and cook another 10 minutes.

3. Reduce the heat to low and cover. Cook 25 minutes, or till rice is done. Stir the pumpkin in during the last 5 minutes of cooking.

4. Turn the heat up to med-high and stir in the cheese. Cook, uncovered, till most of the liquid is gone. Serve immediately garnished with the chopped parsley and additional Parmesan cheese.

Roasted Corn

Make delicious ears of roasted corn using the air fryer! This method cuts down on cooking time and turns out a delicious dish that is perfect for summer barbecues or picnics.

Yields: 4 – 6 servings

Prep Time: 10 minutes

Cook Time: 10 minutes

Ingredients:

- 4 ears of corn, shucked and cut into thirds
- 2 - 3 teaspoons vegetable oil
- salt and pepper to taste

Preparation instructions:

1. Place corn in a large bowl and drizzle with oil. Toss being sure to coat each piece. Sprinkle with salt and pepper.
2. Place the corn in the basket for the air fryer, you may have to cook these in batches. Add the Tender Crisp lid and set the temperature to 400 degrees. Cook 10 minutes. Serve.

Scalloped Pineapple

Scalloped pineapple is a traditional side dish in the South. You can serve it with dinner, it goes great with ham, or you can even serve it as a summer time dessert.

Yields: 8 – 10 servings

Prep Time: 15 minutes

Cook Time: 35 minutes

Ingredients:

- 20 ounce can pineapple tidbits, reserve ¼ cup juice,
- 20 ounce can crushed pineapple, drained
- 40 Ritz crackers, crushed
- 2 cups sharp cheddar cheese, grated
- ½ cup sugar
- ½ cup butter, melted
- 6 tablespoons flour

Preparation instructions:

1. In a mixing bowl, combine all ingredients except the cracker crumbs and the butter.
2. Lightly spray the cooking pot with cooking spray. Add the pineapple mixture.
3. In a small bowl, combine the crackers crumbs and butter. Sprinkle over the top of the pineapple mixture.
4. Add the Tender Crisp lid and set the temperature to 350 degrees. Bake 35 minutes or till top is golden brown. Serve warm.

Soy-Glazed Mushrooms

Tangy mushrooms with a savory glaze goes well with almost any meat recipe. Cook these up to top a steak, pork chops or even chicken for a tasty meal.

Yields: 4 servings

Prep Time: 5 minutes

Cook Time: 10 minutes

Ingredients:

- 2 cups mushrooms, sliced
- 4 tablespoons butter
- 3 cloves garlic, chopped fine
- 1-3 teaspoons soy sauce

Preparation instructions:

1. Set cooker to sauté on med-high heat. Add butter and let melt. Add mushrooms, stirring to coat. Cook till mushrooms release their liquid then add garlic and continue to cook, stirring often, till the liquid has evaporated and the mushrooms are golden brown.
2. Drizzle on desired amount of soy sauce and stir. Serve.

Spicy Red Potatoes

These slow cooked red potatoes are chock full of spicy flavor. Serve them with any Mexican dishes, or whenever you want to spice an otherwise bland piece of chicken or beef.

Yields: 6 – 8 servings

Prep Time: 5 minutes

Cook Time: 3 -4 hours

Ingredients:

- 3 pounds red potatoes, quartered
- 1 packet taco seasoning
- 2 tablespoons olive oil
- 2 tablespoons butter
- 1 tablespoon red pepper flakes
- salt and pepper to taste

Preparation instructions:

1. Spray the cooking pot with cooking spray. Add all of the ingredients and stir well to coat the potatoes.

2. Add the lid and select slow cooking on high. Cook 3-4 hours, stirring the potatoes every hour. At the 3 hour mark check for doneness, when they are fork tender they are done. Serve.

Squash with Cherries

This is a lovely dish that combines two fall favorites. It makes a lovely side dish on your holiday table, or make it to go with a ham dinner in place of the usual sweet potatoes.

Yields: 6 – 8 servings

Prep Time: 10 minutes

Cook Time: 1 hour

Ingredients:

- 3 cups butternut squash, peeled and cut into 1-inch cubes
- 10 slivers lemon peel
- 1 cup apple juice
- 3 cinnamon sticks
- 2 vanilla beans
- ½ cup dried cherries
- ½ teaspoon sea salt

Preparation instructions:

1. Place all ingredients in the cooking pot and toss to combine.
2. Add the Tender Crisp lid and set the temperature to 350 degrees. Bake 45 minutes to 1 hour, or till squash is tender and the top is golden brown. Serve.

Teriyaki Green Beans & Mushrooms

Never serve boring green beans again. This tasty side combines green beans and mushrooms with a tasty teriyaki sauce. It is quick to make which it makes it ideal for a weeknight side dish.

Yields: 4 – 6 servings

Prep Time: 5 minutes

Cook Time: 10 minutes

Ingredients:

- 1 pound fresh green beans, cut into 1-inch pieces
- 1 ¼ cups mushrooms, sliced
- 1 shallot, diced
- ¼ cup teriyaki sauce
- 3 tablespoons butter
- 1 teaspoon garlic, chopped fine
- ½ teaspoon sesame seeds

Preparation instructions:

1. Add butter to the cooker and set to sauté on med-high heat. Once butter melts, add beans, mushrooms and shallot. Cook till the vegetables start to soften, about 4-5 minutes.

2. Add garlic and cook another 30 seconds. Add teriyaki sauce and cook 5 minutes, or till green beans are done. Sprinkle with sesame seeds before serving.

Zucchini Pasta with Walnuts & Basil

Vegetable "noodles" have become quite the rage. They serve the same purpose as pasta but are healthier and lower in fat and calories. This dish combines zucchini noodles with fresh basil and crunchy walnuts, delicious.

Yields: 3 – 4 servings

Prep Time: 90 minutes

Cook Time: 10 minutes

Ingredients:

- 4 large zucchini, peeled
- ½ cup walnuts, chopped
- 1/3 cup bacon grease
- ¼ cup fresh basil, chopped
- 2 cloves garlic, chopped fine
- 2 teaspoons salt

Preparation instructions:

1. If you have a vegetable spiralizer, use it to create zucchini noodles. If you don't, cut the zucchini, lengthwise into long, thin strips that resemble spaghetti noodles. Place in a colander and sprinkle with salt, toss to coat. Place over the kitchen sink for 1 hour to extract the water.

2. Rinse the zucchini thoroughly till no salt remains. Drain on paper towels.

3. Set the cooker to saute on med-high heat and add the bacon grease. Once it is hot, add garlic and zucchini and cook, stirring often, about 4-5 minutes or it is al dente.

4. Stir in basil and walnuts and cook another 2 minutes. Serve.

SOUPS & STEWS

Autumn Stew

This hearty stew will warm you up inside on those chilly fall evenings. It uses many of the root vegetables that are harvested during the fall and the addition of smoked sausage helps pack it full of flavor.

Yields: 4 -6 servings

Prep Time: 15 minutes

Cook Time: 8 hours

Ingredients:

- 1 pound smoked sausage, sliced, not too thin
- 4 potatoes, peeled and quartered
- 3 carrots, peeled and chopped
- 3 stalks celery, sliced
- 2-3 turnips, peeled and cubed
- 1 small cabbage, cut into chunks
- 1 large can of tomatoes, diced
- 1 teaspoon sage
- 1 teaspoon oregano
- 1 teaspoon basil
- ½ teaspoon thyme
- ½ teaspoon rosemary
- Salt & pepper

Preparation instructions:

1. Layer the ingredients in the cooking pot; carrots, turnips, celery, potatoes and cabbage, sprinkling each layer with a little of the herbs, salt and pepper.
2. Spread tomatoes, with liquid, over cabbage and top with sausage. Sprinkle more seasonings on top.
3. Secure the lid and select slow cooking function. The stew will take 7-8 hours on low or 4-5 on high heat. The stew is done with vegetables are tender. Stir well before serving.

Cheesy Onion Soup

After you taste this soup, you may never want the usual onion soup again. Sweet Vidalia onions combined with sharp cheddar cheese and dry white wine takes this onion soup to a new level.

Yields: 4 servings

Prep Time: 10 minutes

Cook Time: 10 minutes

Ingredients:

- 2 ¼ cups sharp cheddar cheese, grated
- 1 Vidalia onion, sliced thin
- 1 can chicken broth
- 1 cup milk
- ¼ cup celery, chopped fine
- ¼ cup dry white wine
- 2 tablespoons butter
- 2 tablespoons flour
- 1 tablespoon chives, chopped
- ½ teaspoon pepper
- ½ teaspoon dry mustard

Preparation instructions:

1. Add butter to the cooking pot and set to sauté on medium heat. Once melted, add onion and celery and cook 3 minutes, stirring often.

2. Stir in flour, pepper and mustard. Slowly stir in the milk, broth and wine. Bring to a boil and cook, stirring, one minute.

3. Stir in the cheese, reduce heat to low and while stirring constantly, cook till cheese is melted. Ladle into bowls and garnish with chopped chives.

Creamy Chicken & Mushroom Soup

Creamy, comforting and best of all quick to make. This cozy soup combines chicken and mushrooms, which make a great pair, with herbs in a cream base. Perfect for warming you up after a long day.

Yields: 6 servings

Prep Time: 15 minutes

Cook Time: 15 minutes

Ingredients:

- 6 chicken thighs, boneless, skinless and cut into 1-inch pieces
- 4 cups chicken broth
- 1 cup cremini mushrooms, sliced thin
- 3 carrots, peeled and chopped fine
- 2 stalks celery, chopped fine
- 1 onion, chopped fine
- ½ cup half-and-half
- ¼ cup flour
- 3 cloves garlic, chopped fine
- 2 tablespoons butter
- 2 tablespoons fresh parsley, chopped
- 1 tablespoon olive oil
- ½ teaspoon thyme
- 1 sprig rosemary
- 1 bay leaf
- Salt & pepper

Preparation instructions:

1. Add the olive oil to the pot and set to sauté on medium heat. Sprinkle the chicken with salt and pepper and add to the pot. Cook till brown, about 2-3 minutes, set aside.
2. Add the butter and let it melt. Once melted, add the vegetables and cook till tender, about 3-4 minutes. Stir in thyme and cook 1 minute more.
3. Stir in flour till lightly browned, about 1 minute. Add the broth, bay leaf, rosemary and chicken and cook, stirring constantly, till soup thickens, about 4-5 minutes.
4. Stir in the half-and-half and continue cooking till heated through, 1-2 minutes. Discard bay leaf and rosemary sprig. Serve immediately.

Duck Ale Chili

Many people are afraid to tackle a duck dish. But, cooking duck is easier than you might think. The secret is to make sure the fat is rendered to bring out all the flavor. Here is an easy duck chili to get your feet wet.

Yields: 6 servings

Prep Time: 10 minutes

Cook Time: 45 minutes

Ingredients:

- 1 ½ pound duck breast
- 1 large can fire roasted tomatoes, diced
- 1 can kidney beans, rinsed and drained
- 1 can great northern beans, rinsed and drained
- 1 bottle brown ale
- 1 small can tomato paste
- 1 cup white onion, chopped fine
- 5 cloves garlic, chopped fine
- 2 tablespoons chili powder
- 1 tablespoon Worcestershire
- 1 tablespoon oregano
- 2 teaspoons cumin
- 1 teaspoon salt
- 1 teaspoon ground black pepper
- 1 teaspoon smoked paprika
- 1 teaspoon onion powder
- 1 teaspoon red pepper flakes
- ½ teaspoon cayenne pepper

Garnishes:

- 1 cup mozzarella cheese, grated
- ½ cup chopped cilantro

Preparation instructions:

1. Score the fat on the duck and sprinkle with salt. Place, fat side down, in the cooking pot.
2. Select sauté on medium heat and sear the duck till golden brown and most of the fat has been rendered. Transfer duck to a plate.
3. Add the onions and cook till they soften, about 5 minutes. Add the duck back to the pot along with remaining ingredients.
4. Secure the lid and set to pressure cooking on high. Set the timer for 30 minutes. When the timer goes off, use manual release to remove the lid.
5. Remove the duck and shred with two forks. Return it to the pot and stir well.
6. Ladle into bowl and top with garnishes before serving.

Greens & Beans Soup

Not only is this healthy turkey and vegetable soup good for you, it may help to ward off cold and flu season. Many of these ingredients have been found to eliminate or prevent many cold and flu symptoms.

Yields: 8 – 10 servings

Prep Time: 10 minutes

Cook Time: 6 hours

Ingredients:

- 1 pound bean soup mix, rinsed and debris removed
- 6 cups chicken broth
- 6 cups mustard or collard greens, chopped
- 2 smoked turkey wings.
- 2 cups baby Portabella mushrooms
- 1 onion, chopped
- 1 can tomatoes, diced
- 1 cup carrots, cut into chunks
- 7 cloves garlic, chopped fine
- ¾ cup red wine
- 2 tablespoons Italian seasoning
- 1 teaspoon sage
- 2 bay leaves
- Salt & pepper

Preparation instructions:

1. Add all of the ingredients, but use only half the greens, to the cooking pot. Secure lid and select slow cooking on high. Cook 5 ½ hours.

2. Remove turkey wings. When cool enough to handle, remove any meat from the bones and add it back to the soup. Add remaining greens and cook another 15 minutes. Serve topped with Parmesan cheese if desired.

Irish Lamb Stew

A traditional Irish stew made with lamb, potatoes, leeks spinach and herbs. Cook it up for St. Patrick's Day in place of the usual corn beef, or just make it any winter night you want a warm hearty meal.

Yields: 6 servings

Prep Time: 15 mins

Cook Time: 8 hours 15 mins

Ingredients:

- 1 ½ pounds lamb stew meat
- 4 cups chicken broth
- 3 ½ cups cabbage, chopped
- 2 cups water
- 2 large potatoes, peeled and chopped
- 1 onion, chopped
- 1 carrot, chopped
- 1 leek, chopped
- 1 cup baby spinach
- 2 tablespoons olive oil
- 1 tablespoon fresh mint, chopped fine
- 2 sprigs rosemary
- 1 bay leaf

Preparation instructions:

1. Add 1 tablespoon of the oil to the cooking pot and set to sauté on medium heat. Sprinkle the lamb with salt and pepper and add to the pot. Cook till brown on both sides, about 8 – 10 minutes. Transfer the lamb to a plate.
2. Add the remaining oil to the pot along with the onion. Cook, stirring often, 2 minutes. Add the carrots and the leek. Cook till the vegetables start to soften, about 5 minutes.
3. Add the potatoes and the lamb to the pot. Pour in the broth and water, then add the rosemary and bay leaf. Secure the lid and select slow cooking on low. Cook 8 hours.
4. Stir in the spinach before serving. Ladle into bowls and sprinkle with mint.

Jamaican Chicken Stew

This recipe is inspired by the traditional Jamaican Brown Stew. This one uses chicken and red bell peppers in a rich, Caribbean brown sauce. It takes a little time to put together but it is worth it.

Yields: 6 servings

Prep Time: 45 mins

Cook Time: 30 mins

Ingredients:

Marinade

- 2 ½ – 3 pounds chicken thighs, skinless
- 1-2 green onions, chopped
- 1 teaspoon garlic, chopped fine
- ½ teaspoon ginger, grated
- ½ teaspoon white pepper
- ½ teaspoon thyme
- ½ teaspoon salt
- ½ teaspoon chicken bouillon powder

For the stew

- 2 cups chicken broth
- 1-2 small red bell peppers, seeded and chopped
- 1 onion, chopped fine
- ¼ cup vegetable oil
- 1 tablespoon ketchup
- 2 teaspoon brown sugar
- 1 teaspoon browning sauce
- 1 teaspoon hot sauce
- 1 teaspoon smoked paprika
- ½ teaspoon thyme
- salt to taste

Preparation instructions:

1. Place chicken in a large bowl, then add all of the marinade ingredients. Mix to make sure the chicken is coated. Cover and refrigerate at least 30 minutes or overnight.

2. When ready to cook shake off any excess spice or onions from the chicken.

3. Add the oil to the cooking pot and set to sauté on medium. When the oil is hot, add the chicken and cook till chicken is browned, about 4-5 minutes. Remove the chicken to a plate and drain off excess oil.

4. Add onions, hot sauce, paprika and bell peppers to the pot. Cook, stirring often, till onion is translucent, about 2-3 minutes. Add the chicken with remaining stew ingredients and bring to a boil. Let it simmer, stirring often, till sauce thickens, about 15-20 minutes.

Lamb Provencal

A rich lamb stew with root vegetables and herbs. This tasty dish will quickly become a favorite in your house. It makes a nice, comforting meal after a cold winter's day.

Yields: 4 servings

Prep Time: 20 minutes

Cook Time: 40 minutes

Ingredients:

- 1 pound lamb stew meat
- 4 cups beef broth
- 2 cups mushrooms, quartered
- 2 cups sweet potatoes, peeled and cubed
- 2 cups turnips, peeled and cubed
- 1 cup dry red wine
- 1 shallot, chopped fine
- ¾ cup flour
- 2 tablespoons olive oil
- 1 tablespoon Herbes de Provence
- 2 bay leaves
- 1 sprig rosemary
- 1 teaspoon garlic, chopped fine
- ½ teaspoon salt
- a few grinds of pepper

Preparation instructions:

1. In a large bowl, mix together flour with some salt and pepper. Add the lamb and toss to coat well.
2. Add the oil to the cooking pot and set to sauté on med-high heat. When hot, add the lamb, shallot and garlic and cook till lamb begins to brown.
3. Add the broth, wine and seasonings and stir to combine. Secure the lid and set to pressure cooking on high. Set the timer for 30 minutes.
4. When the timer goes off, use quick release to remove the lid. Add the vegetables and secure the lid again. Cook on high pressure for 10 minutes.
5. Use quick release to remove the lid. Stir well and serve.

Mushroom & Wild Rice Soup

Mushrooms and wild rice come together in a rich broth in this delicious, earthy soup. This recipe doesn't call for meat but you could easily add some if you want to. Like most soups, it tastes even better the next day.

Yields: 6 servings

Prep Time: 15 minutes

Cook Time: 6 – 8 hours

Ingredients:

- 1 pound mushrooms, halved
- 4 cups beef broth
- 2 carrots, cut into ½-inch pieces
- 1 cup frozen sweet peas, thawed
- 1 cup water
- 1 stalk celery, cut into ½-inch pieces
- ½ cup whole-grain wild rice
- 1 envelope onion soup mix
- 1 tablespoon sugar

Preparation instructions:

1. Layer mushrooms, rice, celery, carrots, soup mix and sugar in the cooking pot. Pour water and broth over top.
2. Add lid and set to slow cooking on low. Cook 5-8 hours.
3. Add the peas during the last 10 minutes of cooking. Serve.

Poblano Beef Stew

Don't let the simplicity of this dish fool you. It is rich and packed with flavor. It makes the perfect meal when paired with warm flour tortillas.

Yields: 4 – 6 servings
Prep Time: 20 minutes
Cook Time: 1 hour
Ingredients:

- 1 ½ pounds beef chuck roast, cut into 1-inch cubes
- 4 cups beef broth
- 15 ounce can fire roasted tomatoes
- 3 large poblano peppers
- 2 potatoes, cut into 1-inch cubes
- 1 onion, chopped
- 2-3 tablespoons cilantro, chopped
- 1 tablespoon olive oil
- 1 tablespoon garlic, chopped fine
- 1 ½ teaspoon ground cumin
- 1 teaspoon oregano

Preparation instructions:

1. Place the poblano chilies in the cooker. Add the Tender Crisp lid and set to broil. Cook the chilies 5-7 minutes, turning a couple of times, till skin is charred. Place them in a bowl and cover with foil. Let sit 10 minutes, then remove the skin. Remove the ribs and seeds and cut into 1-inch pieces.
2. Add the oil to the pot and set to sauté on med-high heat. Sprinkle the beef with salt and pepper and add to the pot, in batches. Cook the beef till no longer pink. Remove and set aside.
3. Add the onions and cook till they are translucent, about 3-5 minutes. Add the garlic and cook another 30 seconds. Add remaining ingredients except the potatoes and cilantro and stir to combine.
4. Secure the lid and set to pressure cooking on high. Set the timer for 40 minutes. When the timer goes off use quick release to remove the lid.
5. Add the potatoes and pressure cook on high another 8-10 minutes. Use quick release again. Stir and ladle into bowls. Top with chopped cilantro before serving.

Sausage & Spinach Stew

This delicious stew is full of Italian flavors. It combines Italian chicken sausage with cannellini, pasta and white wine. And you can have it ready to eat in about 30 minutes!

Yields: 4 servings

Prep Time: 5 minutes

Cook Time: 20 minutes

Ingredients:

- 12 ounce Italian chicken sausage, fully cooked
- 4 cups chicken broth
- 1 bag spinach
- 1 can cannellini beans, rinsed and drained
- 1 cup ditalini pasta
- ½ cup dry white wine
- 4 cloves garlic, chopped
- 1 tablespoon olive oil
- Pepper
- Parmesan cheese

Preparation instructions:

1. Add oil to cooker and set to sauté on medium heat. Add the sausage and cook, stirring often, till brown, about 4-5 minutes. Remove to a plate.

2. Add the garlic and cook, stirring, 1 minute. Add the wine and simmer to deglaze the pan, about 1 minutes.

3. Add the broth and pasta and bring to a boil. Cook till pasta is tender, about 8-10 minutes. Stir in the beans, sausage and pepper and cook till heated through. Turn the cooker off and stir in the spinach. Ladle into bowls and top with Parmesan cheese before serving.

Seafood Stew

This seafood chowder is packed with lobster, shrimp and cod with just a touch of heat. Serve it with toasty bread for an easy weeknight meal.

Yields: 4 servings

Prep Time: 20 mins

Cook Time: 25 mins

Ingredients:

- 1 pound mixed lobster, shrimp and cod
- 3 ½ cups water
- 3 ½ cups tomatoes, crushed
- 2 cups potatoes, cubed
- 1 ½ cups celery, sliced
- 1 ½ cups onions, chopped
- 1 ½ cups carrots, sliced
- ¼ cups shallots, chopped
- 4 - 6 cloves of garlic, chopped fine
- 1 teaspoon salt
- 1 teaspoon pepper
- 1 teaspoon basil
- 1 teaspoon Greek seasoning
- 1 teaspoon Sriracha sauce

Preparation instructions:

1. Place all the vegetables, except the potatoes into the cooking pot. Add tomatoes, water and seasonings. Secure lid and set to pressure cooking on high. Set timer for 10 minutes.

2. When timer goes off, use quick release to remove the lid. Add the potatoes and pressure cook another 8 minutes. Use quick release again.

3. Set to sauté on medium heat. Stir in the seafood and cook till shrimp and lobster is pink and the stew is heated through, about 5 minutes. Serve.

Shrimp & Mango Curry

This Caribbean style curry combines shrimp with mangoes and curry for tasty dish you will want to make again. It has a spicy, sweet kick so the kids may even eat it too.

Yields: 4 servings

Prep Time: 15 minutes

Cook Time: 15 minutes

Ingredients:

- 1 ¼ pounds shrimp, peeled and deveined
- 2 cups clam juice
- 1 can coconut milk
- 3 mangoes, chopped
- 1 onion, chopped
- 2 stalks celery, sliced
- 1 bunch scallions, sliced
- 4 cloves garlic, chopped fine
- 1 serrano chili, seeded and chopped fine
- 2 tablespoons curry powder
- 1 tablespoon olive oil
- 1 teaspoon thyme
- ¼ teaspoon salt

Preparation instructions:

1. Add oil to cooker and set to sauté on medium heat. Add onion and celery and cook, stirring often, till the onion begins to brown, about 3-5 minutes.

2. Add garlic, chili, curry powder and thyme, stir constantly and cook 30 seconds. Add the clam juice, coconut milk and mangoes and increase the heat to med-high. Bring to a simmer and cook, stirring often, for 5 minutes.

3. Add 3 cups of the soup to a blender and process till smooth. Return it to the pot and bring back to simmer. Add shrimp and cook till they turn pink, about 3 minutes. Stir in scallions and salt and serve.

Sunchoke & Asparagus Soup

This low calorie and tasty soup combines sunchokes, or Jerusalem artichokes, with asparagus in a cream a base. It makes a great starter before dinner.

Yields: 4 servings

Prep Time: 30 minutes

Cook Time: 15 minutes

Ingredients:

- 1 pound asparagus, cut off 1 ½ inches of the tips, discard woody ends and chop remaining into 1-inch pieces
- 3 cups vegetable broth
- ½ pound sunchokes, peeled and chopped
- 1 ½ cups potato, peeled and chopped
- 2 large shallots, peeled and sliced
- 2 tablespoons olive oil
- ½ teaspoons salt
- 1/8 teaspoon white pepper

Preparation instructions:

1. Add oil to the pot and set to sauté on medium heat. Add shallot and cook till soft. Add the vegetables along with the broth. Secure the lid and set to pressure cooking on high. Set the timer for 10 minutes. When the timer goes off, use quick release to remove the lid.
2. While the vegetables are cooking, bring a small pot of water to a boil and prepare an ice bath in a bowl. Add the asparagus tips to the boiling water and cook 2 minutes. Transfer the tips to the ice bath with a slotted spoon.
3. Once the vegetables in the cooking pot are tender, use an immersion blender to puree till smooth. Season with salt and pepper to taste.
4. To serve, ladle soup into bowls, divide the asparagus tips among them and drizzle a little olive oil over the top.

Sweet Potato & Black Bean Stew

This hearty stew combines healthy sweet potatoes, kale and black beans with a hint of lime. It makes a satisfying meal whether you eat it for lunch or dinner.

Yields: 6 servings

Prep Time: 10 minutes

Cook Time: 25 minutes

Ingredients:

- 4 cups vegetable broth
- 4 cups kale, chopped
- 3 cups sweet potatoes, peeled and cubed
- 1 can black beans, rinsed and drained
- 1 large onion, chopped
- 4 cloves garlic, chopped fine
- 3 green onions, sliced thin
- 2 radishes, sliced thin
- 2 tablespoons olive oil
- 1 tablespoon lime juice
- 2 teaspoons oregano
- 1 ½ teaspoons cumin
- 1 teaspoon garlic powder
- ½. teaspoon black pepper
- ½ teaspoon salt
- ¼ teaspoon cayenne

Preparation instructions:

1. Add the oil to the pot and set to sauté on med-high heat. Add the onions and cook till translucent, about 3 minutes. Reduce heat to medium, add the garlic and seasonings and cook for 30 seconds.

2. Add the potatoes, broth, beans and salt and bring to a low boil. Cook 15 minutes, or till potatoes are tender.

3. Turn off the heat and stir in kale, green onions and lime juice. Serve.

Tipsy Potato Chowder

This is not your usual potato soup. The addition of beer helps to cut down on the richness while adding just a bit of tang to punch up the flavor.

Yields: 5 servings

Prep Time: 20 minutes

Cook Time: 8 hours

Ingredients:

- 6 cups potatoes, peeled and cubed
- 2 cups cheddar cheese, grated
- 1 ¾ cups chicken broth
- 1 can beer
- ½ cup onion, chopped
- ½ cup celery, chopped
- ½ cup carrot, chopped
- ½ cup heavy cream
- 1 clove garlic, chopped fine
- ¼ teaspoon pepper

Preparation instructions:

1. Combine all ingredients, except the cheese and cream to the cooking pot. Add lid and set to slow cooking on low. Cook 6-8 hours, stirring every so often

2. About 10 minutes before serving, coarsely mash the vegetables, leaving the soup a little chunky. Add cheese and cream and stir to combine. Cover and cook 5 minutes more or till cheese is melted. Serve.

Tuscan-Style Veggie Soup

This pretty soup is inspired by the ones you find in Tuscany. Healthy veggies topped with Parmesan cheese and crunch croutons makes for a delicious light lunch or summer dinner.

Yields: 4 servings

Prep Time: 10 minutes

Cook Time: 20 minutes

Ingredients:

- 3 cups vegetable broth
- 2 cups kale, chopped
- 2 cups croutons
- ½ large can tomatoes, diced
- 1 can navy beans, rinsed and drained
- 1 cup water
- 1 onion, chopped
- ½ cup fresh basil, chopped
- ½ cup Parmesan cheese
- 1 tablespoon olive oil
- 1 clove garlic, chopped fine

Preparation instructions:

1. Add oil to the pot and set cooker to sauté on medium heat. Add the onion and garlic and cook, stirring often, 3 minutes. Add the broth, water, beans and tomatoes. Bring to a boil, then reduce heat to med-low.
2. Cover and cook 10 minutes. Stir in the kale and cook 5 minutes more or till kale is tender.
3. Ladle into bowls and top with croutons and Parmesan cheese.

Venison Stew

This rich, hearty stew combines venison with bacon. Venison can be found at specialty butcher shops, unless you happen to know someone who enjoys hunting. If you can't find venison, then you can substitute beef instead.

Yields: 4 servings

Prep time: 10 mins

Cook time: 2 hours

Ingredients:

- 1 pound venison stew meat
- 3 cups beef broth
- 4 slices bacon, cut into ½-inch pieces
- 1 cup dry red wine
- 2 carrots, sliced
- 1 large potato, cubed
- 1 onion, chopped
- 1 stalk celery, sliced thin
- ½ cup cold water
- 3 tablespoons flour
- ½ teaspoon salt
- ¼ teaspoon thyme
- ¼ teaspoon marjoram
- ¼ teaspoon pepper

Preparation instructions:

1. Add the bacon to the pot and set cooker to sauté on med-high heat. Cook till crispy, remove to paper towel lined plate.
2. Add the venison to the pot and cook till brown on all sides. Add the broth, wine, celery, carrots and seasonings and stir to combine. Add the lid and set the cooker to slow cooking on high. Cook one hour.
3. After one hour, add the potatoes and cook till meat and vegetables are tender.
4. Stir the flour into the cold water in a small bowl, or measuring glass. Stir into the stew and continue to cook thill thickened, about 5-10 minutes. Stir in bacon just before serving.

Verde Pork Stew

Tender pork loin, fire roasted tomatoes and a green chili sauce make this stew simply divine. You could serve it garnished with grated cheese and sour cream with warm tortillas, cornbread or just add to some toasted hoagie rolls for a delicious sandwich.

Yields: 6 servings

Prep Time: 5 minutes

Cook Time: 4 – 8 hours

Ingredients:

- 1 – 1 ½ pound pork tenderloin
- 2 cups chicken broth
- 1 16-ounce jar salsa verde
- 1 15-ounce can black beans, rinsed and drained
- 1 teaspoon cumin

Preparation instructions:

1. Place all ingredients in the cooking pot. Set to slow cooker functions. Cook 3-4 hours on high heat, or 6-8 hours on low.

2. When pork is tender, transfer it to a bowl and shred with two forks. Return it to the pot and stir to combine. Serve garnished as desired.

White Chicken Chili

Hearty chili with chicken, beans and green chilies. This delicious chili is perfect on cold winter days to warm you inside and out. If you do not like spicy food, reduce the amount of cayenne pepper and cumin by half.

Yields: 6-8 servings

Prep Time: 15 minutes

Cook Time: 40-50 minutes

Ingredients:

- 4 cups chicken, cooked and chopped
- 3 ½ cups chicken broth
- 2 cans white beans, drained and rinsed
- 2 cans green chilies, diced
- 1 onion, chopped
- 2 teaspoons olive oil
- 2 teaspoons cumin
- 2 teaspoons oregano
- 1 clove garlic, chopped fine
- 1 teaspoon cayenne pepper

Preparation Instructions:

1. Set cooker to sauté on med-high heat and add oil. Once oil is hot, add onion and cook 3-4 minutes or they are translucent. Add garlic and cook another minute. Add green chilies and spices and cook 2 more minutes, stirring frequently.

2. Add broth and beans. Secure lid. Set to pressure cooking function with low pressure. Set timer for 20 minutes. When timer goes off, use quick release to remove the lid.

3. Set back to sauté on low heat. Add chicken and cook 10-15 minutes, stirring occasionally. Serve garnished as desired.

DESSERTS

Banana Bundt Cake

This moist cake combines ripe bananas with honey and cinnamon. Use a bundt cake pan that will fit inside the cooker, 6-8 inches will work. You can serve it dusted with powdered sugar or glaze it if you prefer.

Yields: 4 -6 servings

Prep Time: 5 minutes

Cook Time: 30 minutes

Ingredients:

- 1 cup flour
- 1 ripe banana, mashed
- 1/3 cup brown sugar, packed
- ¼ cup butter, soft
- 1 egg
- 2-3 tablespoons walnuts, chopped
- 2 tablespoons honey
- ½ teaspoon cinnamon
- Pinch of salt

Preparation instructions:

1. Preheat air fryer to 320 degrees. Lightly spray a small ring cake pan with cooking spray.
2. Place the butter and sugar in a mixing bowl and beat till creamy. Add egg, banana and honey and stir till smooth.
3. Add the dry ingredients and stir to mix well. Pour into prepared pan.
4. Add the rack to the bottom of the cooking pot and place pan on it. Add the Tender Crisp lid and bake 30 minutes or it passes the toothpick test.
5. Carefully remove the pan from the cooker and let cool 10 minutes before transferring to a serving plate. Garnish if desired.

Bananas Foster

Bananas Foster is traditionally served tableside in a fancy restaurant. It is a dessert that impresses with both its flavor and the fact is it usually set on fire before serving, please do not try that at home.

Yields: 6 – 8 servings

Prep Time: 5 minutes

Cook Time: 2 hours

Ingredients:

- 7 bananas, not too ripe, sliced into ½-inch pieces
- 6 tablespoons honey
- Juice of 1 lemon
- 2 tablespoons coconut oil, melted
- 1 teaspoon rum extract
- ½ teaspoon cinnamon

1 tablespoon coconut oil, melted (unrefined coconut oil)

3 tablespoon honey

Juice from 1/2 lemon

1/4 teaspoon cinnamon

5 bananas, medium firmness, 1/2" slices

1/2 teaspoon 100% Rum Extract (optional)

Preparation instructions:

1. Add the coconut oil, honey, lemon juice and cinnamon to the cooking pot. Stir to combine. Add bananas and toss gently to coat. Add the lid and set to slow cooking on low. Cook 1 ½ - 2 hours.

2. Just before serving, add the rum extract. Serve over vanilla ice cream, or topped with whip cream.

Blackberry Brioche Bread Pudding

This simple bread pudding is oozing with warm blackberries. Top it with fresh whip cream or serve it with a big scoop of vanilla ice cream, delicious.

Yields: 4-6 servings

Prep Time: 5 minutes

Cook Time: 30 – 46 minutes

Ingredients:

- 4 cups brioche bread cubes, loosely packed
- ½ pint blackberries, rinse and pat dry
- 1 cup milk
- 2 eggs
- ½ cup sugar
- 1 teaspoon vanilla
- pinch of salt

Preparation instructions:

1. Lightly spray the cooking pot with cooking spray.
2. Place the bread cubes and berries in the pot.
3. In a mixing bowl, whisk remaining ingredients together and pour over the bread and berries.
4. Add the Tender Crisp lid and set to 350 degrees. Bake 45 minutes, or till the pudding puffs up and is starting to brown on top. Serve warm.

Blueberry & Peach Streusel Pie

A delicious combination of juicy peaches and plump blueberries. Instead of a second pie crust on top, this recipe makes a crunchy, sweet streusel topping.

Yields: 6-8 servings
Prep Time: 15 minutes
Cook Time: 20 - 35 minutes
Ingredients:
- 1 pie crust
- 3 peaches, peeled and sliced
- 1 ½ cups fresh blueberries, rinsed & dried
- 2-3 tablespoons tapioca, quick cooking
- 1 ½ tablespoons honey
- 1 tablespoon lemon zest
- 1 tablespoon lemon juice
- 1 egg white, lightly beaten
- 1 ½ teaspoons vanilla
- 1 teaspoon cinnamon

Streusel Topping:
- ½ cup butter, cubed
- ½ cup quick cooking oats
- ½ cup sugar
- ¼ cup flour
- ¼ cup almonds, chopped

Preparation instructions:
1. Preheat air fryer to 340 degrees. Lightly oil a ceramic pie plate that fits inside the cooker.
2. Add the fruit, spices, zest, juice and tapioca to a large bowl and stir well.
3. Add the topping ingredients to a bowl and mix with a fork, or pastry cutter, till it comes together.
4. Roll the pie crust out, or if store bought, unfold it into the prepared pan. Brush the entire crust with the egg white. Add the fruit mixture and spread evenly.
5. Sprinkle the topping over the fruit. Add the rack to the cooking pot and place the pie on it. Bake 20-35 minutes and the crust is cooked. Cool and serve.

Caramel Apple Chimichangas

This delightful dessert is a combination of apple pie wrapped up in a crisp tortilla shell. Since it is made in the air fryer there is less fat and calories, so less guilt.

Yields: 1 dozen

Prep time: 10 mins

Cook time: 6 mins

Ingredients:

- 12 10-inch flour tortillas
- 7 Granny Smith apples, peeled, cored and sliced
- 1 lemon, juice and zest
- ¾ cup light brown sugar
- ¼ cup flour
- ¾ teaspoon ground cinnamon
- Cinnamon sugar
- Caramel sauce

Preparation instructions:

1. Preheat air fryer to 400 degrees.
2. Mix the brown sugar, flour and cinnamon together in small bowl.
3. In a large bowl, toss the apples with the lemon juice, then stir in the sugar mixture making sure to coat all of the apples.
4. Warm the tortillas so they are soft enough to fold. Place ½ - ¾ cup apples in the center of tortilla and fold like a burrito. You can seal the edge with water or use toothpicks.
5. Lightly spray the outsides with cooking spray and sprinkle with the cinnamon sugar.
6. Cook them in batches in the fryer, 6-7 minutes, turning halfway through.
7. Drizzle with the caramel sauce, or serve them with the caramel sauce for dipping.

Cherry Cobbler

This tasty cobbler looks, and tastes, like you spent all afternoon making it. But using the slow cooker function of your Ninja Foodi makes it super simple to throw it together in the afternoon, and it will be ready to serve after dinner.

Yields: 10 – 12 servings

Prep Time: 5 minutes

Cook Time: 5 – 8 hours

Ingredients:

- 1 box yellow cake mix
- 2 cans cherry pie filling
- ½ cup butter, melted
- ½ cup almonds, sliced and toasted
- 1 tablespoon water

Preparation instructions:

1. Lightly spray the cooking pot with cooking spray.
2. Dump the pie filling into the pot. Sprinkle the cake mix over the cherries then add the almonds.
3. Drizzle the melted butter over the top. Using knife, cut through the ingredients to marble them do not mix. Sprinkle water over the top.
4. Place 2-3 paper towels over the cooker then add the lid. Set to slow cooking. The cobbler will be done in 3-5 hours on high, or 5-8 hours on low. Cobbler is done with the cake parts are set but not sticky. Serve warm.

Chocolate Pecan Pie

This recipe takes ordinary pecan pie to a whole new level. The addition of chocolate chips and coconut makes it resemble a German chocolate cake, but it's a pie!

Yields: 8 – 10 servings

Prep Time: 5 mins

Cook Time: 35 minutes

Ingredients:

- 1 pie crust
- 1 cup corn syrup
- 1 cup semisweet chocolate chips
- 1 cup coconut
- 1 cup pecans, chopped
- 3 eggs
- 1/3 cup sugar
- 1/3 cup brown sugar, packed
- 1/3 cup butter, melted
- 1 teaspoon vanilla
- ¼ teaspoon salt

Preparation instructions:

1. Unfold the pie crust into a pie plate that fits inside the cooking pot. Place the rack on the bottom of the pot.

2. In a mixing bowl, combine eggs, syrup, sugars, butter, vanilla and salt.

3. Layer the chocolate chips, coconut and pecans on the bottom of the pie crust. Pour the egg mixture evenly on top. Cover the pastry edge with foil and place the pie on the rack in the pot.

4. Add the Tender Crisp lid and set to 350 degrees. Bake 20 minutes then remove the foil and bake another 15 minutes or till set. Carefully remove from the pot and cool completely.

Coconut Cream Cake

A moist rich cake with plenty of coconut flavor. Bake one up for someone's birthday, Easter or anytime you just want to enjoy the delicious taste.

Yields: 8 – 10 servings

Prep Time: 5 minutes

Cook Time: 35 – 45 minutes

Ingredients:

- 1 box vanilla cake mix
- 1 box instant coconut pudding
- 1 ½ cups coconut
- 1 cup sour cream
- 1 cup coconut milk, unsweetened
- 4 eggs
- ½ cup coconut oil
- 2 teaspoons coconut extract

Glaze

- 1 cup powdered sugar
- Enough milk for the desired consistency

Preparation instructions:

1. Lightly spray a Bundt cake pan that will fit inside the cooking pot with cooking spray.
2. In a large mixing bowl, beat together all ingredients except the coconut. Stir the coconut in by hand.
3. Pour the batter into the prepared pan and lower into the cooking pot. Add the Tender Crisp lid and set the temperature to 320 degrees. Bake 35 – 40 minutes or till it passes the toothpick test.
4. Carefully remove the cake from the pot and let cool 10 minutes. Transfer to a serving plate.
5. Make the glaze, and toast some additional coconut for garnish. Drizzle the glaze over the cake and top with toasted coconut.

Hot Fudge Cake

Making this cake is like working magic! All the ingredients start out combined but during the baking process a rich, hot fudge sauce forms on the top.

Yields: 6 servings

Prep Time: 5 minutes

Cook Time: 2 – 2 ½ hours

Ingredients:

- 1 ½ cups hot water
- 1 cup flour
- ¾ cup brown sugar, packed
- ½ cup sugar
- ½ cup milk
- ½ cup nuts, chopped
- ¼ cup baking cocoa
- 2 tablespoons baking cocoa
- 2 tablespoons vegetable oil
- 2 teaspoons baking powder
- 1 teaspoon vanilla
- ½ teaspoon salt

Preparation instructions:

1. Lightly spray the pot with cooking spray.
2. In a medium bowl mix flour, sugar, 2 tablespoons cocoa, baking powder and salt together. Stir in milk, oil and vanilla till smooth. Stir in nuts and spread the batter evenly in the cooking pot.
3. In a small bowl, whisk together brown sugar, ¼ cup cocoa and hot water till smooth. Pour over batter in the cooking pot.
4. Add the lid and select slow cooking on high. Cook the cake 2 – 21/2 hours or it passes the toothpick test.
5. Turn off the cooker and let the cake rest, uncovered 30-40 minutes. Serve.

Individual S'Mores Pies

No more waiting for that summer camping trip to enjoy the great taste of S'Mores. This petite pies have all the same ingredients and cook up nice and crispy in the air fryer.

Yields: 6 – 12 pies

Prep Time: 10 minutes

Cook Time: 10 minutes

Ingredients:

- 2 sheets of puff pastry, thawed
- 2 chocolate bars
- 1 cup mini marshmallows
- ½ cup graham cracker crumbs
- 1 egg, lightly beaten

Preparation instructions:

1. Roll out the pastry dough on a lightly floured surface. Cut into 2-3 inch squares, or the size you desire.

2. In the center of half the squares, place a piece of chocolate, some marshmallows and graham crumbs. Moisten the edges of the pastry with water and add the remaining squares on top. Press the edges together. Brush the tops with egg wash.

3. Place 2-3 pies in the air fryer basket at a time, add the Tender Crisp lid and set the temperature to 330 degrees. Bake 5-7 minutes or till the outside is puffed and golden brown. Cool slightly before serving. You can drizzle the tops with melted chocolate or melted marshmallow cream.

Lemon Sponge Pie

This Lemon Sponge Pie is an easy pie recipe with refreshing lemon flavor and light and airy texture. It makes a deliciously light treat.

Yields: 8 servings

Prep Time: 15 minutes

Cook Time: 35 – 40 minutes

Ingredients:

- 1 pie crust
- 1 ½ cups sugar
- 1 cup milk
- 2/3 cups lemon juice
- 1/3 cup flour
- 3 eggs, separated
- ¼ teaspoon salt

Preparation instructions:

1. Place the rack in the bottom of the cooking pot. Unfold the pie crust into a pie pan that fits inside the pot.
2. In a large mixing bowl, beat egg whites till stiff peaks form, set aside.
3. In a separate mixing bowl, beat yolks, lemon juice and milk till combined. Add sugar, flour and salt and beat till smooth.
4. Fold lemon mixture into egg whites, until thoroughly blended. Pour into pie crust. Carefully lower the dish onto the rack in the pot. Add the Tender Crisp lid and set temperature to 330 degrees. Bake 35-40 minutes, or till golden brown.
5. Carefully remove the pie from the pot and cool completely. Cover loosely and refrigerate till the filling sets. Serve.

Meyer Lemon Hand Pies

These delicate mini pies are bursting with the bright, tangy flavor of Meyer Lemons. They are ideal for taking on a picnic, serving at a backyard pool party or anytime you are craving the taste of summer.

Yields: 6 servings

Prep Time: 15 minutes

Cook Time: 30 minutes

Ingredients:

- 1 package refrigerated pie dough
- 1 egg, beaten

Lemon Curd

- 4 Meyer lemons, juiced
- 8 egg yolks
- 1 ¾ cups sugar
- ½ cup butter, cold and sliced
- 2 tablespoons lemon zest
- Pinch of salt

Icing

- 1 cup powdered sugar
- ½ lemon

Preparation instructions:

1. Place rack in the middle of the cooking pot and add 1-2 inches of water. Set the cooker to saute on med-high heat and bring to a simmer.

2. Place the yolks and sugar into a bowl that fits inside the pot but is large enough for mixing in, and whisk vigorously till smooth. Add the juice and salt and whisk till smooth again.

3. Once the water reaches a simmer, reduce the heat to med-low and place the bowl on the rack. Cook, whisking constantly, 20-22 minutes, it should be a light yellow color, do not let it boil. Remove from heat and whisk in the zest.

4. Add butter, one piece at a time, and whisk to combine after each addition. Let cool. Transfer to an airtight container and refrigerate overnight.

5. When ready to make the pies, unfold the pie crust on a lightly floured surface. Roll to a ¼-inch thickness. Use a cookie cutter to cut out 6 circles and place them on a baking sheet. Place 1 tablespoon of the lemon curd in the center of each circle and brush the edges with beaten egg. Fold dough over the filling using a fork to seal the edges. Brush the top of the pies with beaten egg and sprinkle sugar over.

6. Place pies, 2 at a time, in the basket of the air fryer. Add the Tender Crisp lid and set the temperature to 380 degrees. Bake 8-10 minutes, or till golden brown. Let pies cool.

7. Place the powdered sugar in a small bowl and whisk in lemon juice till desired consistency. Drizzle over cooled pies and let sit till the glaze sets. Serve.

Noodle Kugel

This noodle pudding is a Jewish tradition for the holidays. The sweet custard has chunks of juicy peaches, raisins and cinnamon and, yes, it has noodles too.

Yields: 10 servings

Prep Time: 20 mins

Cook Time: 6 hours

Ingredients:

- 1 pound egg noodles, uncooked
- 1 bag frozen peaches, thawed and chopped
- 1 can coconut milk
- 1 cup sugar
- 3 eggs
- ¼ cup raisins
- 3 tablespoons orange liquor
- 2 teaspoons cinnamon

Preparation instructions:

1. Soak raisins in the liquor in a small bowl for 20 minutes.
2. Lightly spray the pot with cooking spray. Add milk, sugar, 1 teaspoon cinnamon and eggs to the pot and stir to combine.
3. Add the noodles, raisins with liquor and peaches to the egg mixture and stir to combine. Sprinkle the remaining teaspoon of cinnamon on the top. Add the lid and set slow cooking on low heat. Cook 6 hours.

Pineapple Pecan Bread Pudding

This decadent bread pudding is the perfect finish to any meal. Bright pops of pineapple along with crunchy pecans all baked up in warm goodness.

Yields: Serves 4

Prep Time: 5 minutes

Cook Time: 30 – 35 minutes

Ingredients:

- 2 cups French bread, cubed
- 14 ounce can crushed pineapple, drained
- 1 cup sugar
- ½ cup butter, soft
- 4 eggs
- ¼ cup pecans, chopped
- ½ teaspoon cinnamon

Preparation instructions:

1. Butter a 1 ½ quart baking dish that fits inside the cooking pot. Add the rack to the bottom of the pot.
2. In a large bowl, on medium speed, beat butter sugar and cinnamon for 1 minutes, scraping sides of the bowl frequently. Add eggs and beat 2 minutes, or till light and fluffy. Fold in remaining ingredients and pour into prepared baking dish.
3. Place the dish on the rack and add the Tender Crisp lid. Set the temperature to 330 degrees and bake 30-35 minutes, or it passes the toothpick test. Serve warm dusted with powdered sugar.

Reece's Cookie Bars

Ooey, gooey, cookie bars full of butterscotch and chocolate, yummy. And since they are made in the Ninja Foodi, you don't have to heat up the house to make them.

Yields: 8-10 bars

Prep Time: 2 minutes

Cook Time: 1-2 hours

Ingredients:

- 1 1/3 cup graham cracker crumbs
- 1 cup chocolate chips
- 1 cup peanut butter chips
- 1 can sweetened condensed milk
- ½ cup butter, melted

Preparation instructions:

1. In a small bowl, mix together cracker crumbs and butter.
2. Spray cooker with cooking spray. Press cracker mixture on the bottom. Pour milk over crust then sprinkle both chips over the milk.
3. Add lid and select slow cooking on high. Set timer for 1 hour. Bars are done with edges are golden brown. Let cool then cut into bars.

Super Simple Chocolate Brownies

Who doesn't love a fudgy chocolate brownie? This recipe uses only 5 simple ingredients and since its slow cooker you don't need to heat up the kitchen.

Yields: 6-8 brownies

Prep Time: 2 minutes

Cook Time: 1-2 hours

Ingredients:

- 1 ¼ cups semi-sweet chocolate chips
- 1 cup sugar
- 1 cup flour
- ½ cup butter
- 2 eggs + 1 egg yolk, room temperature

Preparation instructions:

1. Spray cooker with cooking spray.

2. Melt chocolate chips and butter in a large glass bowl. Add sugar and beat well. Beat in eggs, egg yolk and lastly, flour, just till combined.

3. Pour into cooker. Add lid and select slow cooking on high. Set timer for 1 hour. Brownies are done when batter is set and edges look done. Cool cut into bars.

Turtle Fudge Pudding

Once you make this rich, chocolatey dessert, the kids will be begging you to make it again. Rich chocolate, gooey caramel and crunchy pecans come together in one delicious pudding that you make with the slow cooker.

Yields: 6 servings

Prep Time: Less than 5 minutes

Cook Time: 2 ½ - 3 hours

Ingredients:

- 1 2/3 cups hot water
- 1 ½ cups Bisquick
- 1 cup sugar
- ¾ cup caramel topping
- ½ cup unsweetened baking cocoa
- ½ cup milk
- ½ cup pecans, chopped

Preparation instructions:

1. Place rack in the bottom of the cooking pot. Lightly spray a deep baking dish that will fit inside the cooker.

2. In a large bowl, mix Bisquick, ½ cup sugar and the cocoa till combined. Stir in milk and ½ the caramel till well blended. Pour into prepared baking dish and lower on to the rack.

3. Pour the hot water over the top of the chocolate mixture and sprinkle with the remaining ½ cup sugar.

4. Add the lid and set to slow cooking on low. Cook 2 ½ - 3 hours or the top springs back when lightly touched. Turn off the cooker and let stand, uncovered 20 minutes. Serve warm drizzled with remaining caramel and sprinkle with pecans.

www.ingramcontent.com/pod-product-compliance
Lightning Source LLC
Chambersburg PA
CBHW081417080526
44589CB00016B/2572